Early
Fleming County
Kentucky Pioneers

Early
Fleming County
Kentucky Pioneers

WADE COOPER

Commonwealth Book Company
St. Martin, Ohio

ISBN: 978-1-948986-15-1

COVER PHOTOGRAPH: Covered bridge at Goddard, east of
Flemingsburg, Fleming County, Kentucky.

DEDICATION

To my loving wife

Virginia Ellis Hart Cooper

without whose help

this wouldn't be complete

and

Mary Marshall Cooper

my devoted daughter

WADE COOPER was born at Smiles, also called Brushy Fork in Rowan County, Kentucky, on February 3, 1908, the youngest of ten children. His parents were Seth Cooper of Rowan and Laura Bell Elam of Jacobs, Carter County. At the age of six weeks on March 11, 1908, he with his family moved to Fleming County on Flemingsburg R.R. 1, where he spent his childhood and attended the local schools.

After three years in the United States Army, serving in Panama and the Hawaiian Islands as a Non-Commissioned Officer, he was honorably discharged and returned to Fleming County where he resumed his trade of barbering, owning his own shop for a number of years. On June 4, 1935, he married Virginia Ellis Hart and lived on a farm about five miles from Flemingsburg where he raised Hereford cattle, Palomino horses, tobacco, wheat, and corn. They were the parents of one child, Mary Marshall Cooper, a devoted and loving daughter, He was also a licensed Kentucky Real Estate Broker and Auctioneer. After working for the U.S. Government as a Civil Service Employee for thirty years, he retired in 1968.

Following an accident in 1965, he was forced to give up much of his work. For that reason he pursued his hobby of the history of Fleming County and the early settlers in this part of the state, which resulted in the publication of this book in 1974.

Contents

PREFACE

The information in this book was meant to be used as clues but the only proof of accuracy is that the biographical sketches were taken from early newspaper clippings, interviews with descendants of some of these people and the 1884 Atlas of Fleming County, Kentucky.

The intentions of this writer was to put into print the history of Fleming County, Kentucky according to records he has had in his hands for a number of years and to honor the brave pioneers of this section of Kentucky, both men and women who came to make their homes and rear their families when this was a vast wilderness. Out of this wilderness has been carved some of the best farms of Kentucky. Their descendants are honorable men and women in the various business fields.

It is also the desire of the writer that these descendants might have a more vivid picture of their ancestoral homes through this collection of writings.

—*The Author, 1974*

CHAPTER ONE

FLEMING COUNTY, KENTUCKY AND THE MAN IT WAS NAMED FOR

On the first day of June, 1798, by act of the Kentucky Legislature, Fleming County was created, Mason County furnishing the territory out of which it was formed. In like manner, but by acts of the Virginia Legislature, Mason County had been carved from Bourbon County; Bourbon County from Fayette, Fayette from "Kentucky County," then (1780) the most western division of the Colony of Virginia. Thus tracing backward the history of Fleming County, we find she is the great - great - great granddaughter of the "Mother of Presidents"; that in Colonial times gave to the Cause of Freedom a Patrick Henry, whose bold speeches and matchless eloquence roused the Colonists to resist British oppression; Jefferson, who wrote the Declaration of Independence and a Washington, who led the Patriots to victory; and that gave the new Republic its first President whose name its capitol bears. Thus Fleming County has a rich heritage.

The first settlers of the County were the bold, hardy Anglo-Saxon sons of Virginia, with a few enterprising Dutchmen and adventurous Irishmen from Pennsylvania and the Carolinas.

COL. JOHN FLEMING

And the History of Fleming County, Kentucky Which Was Named In His Honor

Fleming Station, Creek, County and Burg are names which point back to a man who must have stood prominently connected with the early settlement and life of the region now called Flemingsburg, Kentucky.

Col. John Fleming is the man to whom these names refer. It is quite natural then, that we should desire to know something of him; but living at a distance of more than

180 years after him, it is exceedingly difficult to learn a great deal about him, either before or after his arrival in Kentucky.

Col. Fleming was born in the State of Virginia, but at what time the writer cannot ascertain. It is supposed that Col. Fleming was induced to come to Kentucky by his half-brother, Major George Stockton. George Stockton was captured by the Indians in Virginia when a child, with a sister, and by them taken to New York and there remained until he became attached to the Indian mode of living. After he was grown, coming with his tribe on a trading expedition into Pennsylvania and knowing that he was not far from his friends and family, he determined, notwithstanding his love of Indian life, to leave them and go back to his old friends in Virginia. Stockton planned his escape from the Indians in a very smooth and intelligent way. He would take short hunting trips each day, and each time he would go a little farther into the woods. Stockton, knowing that the Indians would not trail him after dark, started his hunting trip late in the afternoon. When it was time for his return to camp he was several miles away, and by morning he was at a safe distance from the camp. It is not known how long it took him to make the trip, but he was several days. He suffered no harm as he was accustomed to life in the wilderness. At last George Stockton was again at home with his old friends and kindred. But a fondness for forest life had so intertwined itself in his nature, that he was not contented with what seemed to him the dull uniformity of Virginia life, so he soon set out for Kentucky where he might enjoy the unrestricted freedom of forest life, inducing Col. Fleming, his half-brother, to go with him.

Descending the Ohio River in a canoe, they reached what is now Fleming County, Kentucky in 1787, where Stockton built his station in sight of what is now the city of Flemingsburg. Major Stockton died at the station in 1818.

Col. Fleming continued on to Strodes Station on the north fork of Licking River, at the mouth of Strodes Run (now Clark County) where he made his home for about three years, and while there he married the widow of John Donaldson. Donaldson was shot through the head by an Indian during the excitement attending an effort of the Indians to capture his daughter, who had left the fort to go to the spring for water.

In the year of 1790, Col. Fleming settled Fleming Station, where he remained until his death which was in 1794. When he settled Fleming Station there was but one other settlement, Stockton's Station, in the bounds of what is now Fleming County. Cassidy's Station was settled a short time after this. Stockton's Station was in sight of Flemingsburg, and Cassidy's about one mile and a half north of the line connecting Fleming's and Stockton's.

Remembering that these three Stations were only the small nuclei of Fleming County, we can understand how all of that outlying region now occupied by the communities of Mt. Carmel, Poplar Plains, Tilton and Sherburne with all the territory lying east and south of points toward the mountains, was once one vast wilderness where buffalos, bears, elks, deer, wolves, wild turkeys, grouse and quail by the millions lived in their native freedom. Nor were there any settlements toward the Ohio River nearer than the vicinity of Washington and Strode's Station in Mason County (not to be confused with Strode's in Clark County).

Col. Fleming was the first man that owned over a thousand acres of land in Fleming County (some records show him to be the owner of as much as six thousand acres of land but as a fact I cannot say). The site chosen by Col. Fleming for his Fort was a beautiful mound in the bend of Fleming Creek, which runs south and then changes its course to the west. Upon the level summit area of this elevation, which is about one hundred and fifty feet and about one-half mile from Martha Mills, was erected the fort, consisting of strongly-built log cabins arranged in the form of a square, with an open court or yard inside the square. The walls of the houses were pierced with port holes enabling the settlers to fire upon attacking Indians. This site and burial ground later was a part of the Grannis and

Summers farms.

In Col. Fleming's day, and for some time afterwards, the surrounding forests were infested with Indians, so that it was necessary to be always prepared for their attacks. Two men from the three neighboring stations who were dressed as Indians kept the settlers informed as to the whereabouts of the Indians and gave the alarm in case of attack. One of these scouts was killed by mistake near Cassidy's Station. The men who lived in these stations were in the habit of taking their guns with them to the fields as they never knew when they might be attacked. One of the children was usually detailed to watch while older children worked.

The settlers in Col. Fleming's time knew nothing of the use of sugar and coffee, and other such things as we are now accustomed to think indispensable. Salt was used little in their cooking. The meats secured by hunting were prepared by a method known as "jerking" without salt. The first salt was obtained, it is supposed, from the Upper Blue Licks in Fleming County. A great many buffalo tracks were found leading to the Licks. In those days not a great amount of milk and butter were used, hence a very fine gum spring about one hundred and fifty yards from the Fort was regarded as quite valuable to the Station. This gum spring was connected by means of a subterranean brook with another spring at the foot of the hill near the bank of Fleming Creek. A bundle of flax once dropped into the gum spring, came out at the lower spring.

Col. Fleming was a man of intrepid courage. In the year of 1791 some twenty Indians, having stolen horses and capturing two children near Strode's Station in Clark County, were pursued by about fifteen whites and overtaken on a creek, since called Battle Run, in Fleming County. A sharp contest ensued with equal losses on both sides, but the whites were forced to give way. In this engagement Col. Fleming was severely wounded, so that in the retreat which the whites were forced to make, he was about to be passed. Just as one of his comrades was flying past him in the

20

hurried retreat and seeing an Indian rapidly gaining on him, he directed his friend to point his gun at the Indian and force hm to stop until he could load his gun. The man replied that his gun was not loaded, to which Fleming quickly replied, "The Indian does not know that." He did as he was directed and Fleming's idea worked.

Dr. Fleming, a grandson of Col. Fleming, in later years was describing his grandfather as was told to him by an older lady, a Mrs. Hammonds, who had known Col. Fleming well. In describing the Colonel, she said that he was "rather spare built, about six feet tall, blue eyes, very active and resolute, delighting in the active sports of the day, particularly dancing. "We girls," added the old lady, "used to call him Beau Fleming. He was so polite and gentlemanly." He was also a generous man for the above lady stated that he would frequently "swap" a valuable piece of land for a scrub of a horse, and has been known to give the horse to some friend who in his opinion needed it worse than he needed it.

He had three children, all boys. They were William P., who was a lawyer representing the County in both Houses of the Legislature, and died while in the Senate at Frankfort in the year of 1834; John D., who was a farmer and lived and died near Fleming Station; and Thomas W., who was a merchant in Flemingsburg in his younger days where he resided; in later life, he was a farmer. A large and respectable progeny, bearing the name of Fleming, with others of various names are now living in Fleming County.

Col. Fleming died at an early day, in 1794, and it was necessary that his grave should be immediately obliterated in order to prevent the prowling Indians from exhuming and mutilating the remains. He was buried near the Station on what is now a well-improved farm belonging to Mrs. Virginia Hart Cooper according to the stories related to her by her great-grandmother, whose father, George Summers owned a part of this land. At that time several graves were in the garden to the east of the Summers home. This farm was sold, and not in the Summers family for several years.

When it was bought in 1918 by Virginia Cooper's mother, a great-granddaughter of George Summers, all trace of these graves were gone. At the time this land was owned by George Summers, there was an Indian mound opened. Virginia Cooper has in her possession several heirlooms of the Indian relics taken from this Indian mound. In later years several attempts have been made to locate Fleming's grave, but the actual spot of the grave is not marked, nor is it known. The sons and grandsons made frequent efforts to locate this site, at one time accompanied by Col. Thomas Jones and Thomas Sweet, who were at the burial. But time has obliterated all traces, and other bodies were afterward buried near by, so that it is now impossible to identify the last resting place of this man, who may be called the Father of Fleming County, Kentucky.

CHAPTER TWO

MICHAEL CASSIDY — THE AMAZING IRISHMAN

No person is more intimately connected with the history of Fleming County, Kentucky than the subject of this sketch. Michael Cassidy was born Oct. 22, 1755 in Dublin, Ireland. While he and his brother, Andrew, were attending school, their father sent them money by a relative to defray their expenses and gave orders that it was not to be given to Michael, but was to be placed in the hands of Andrew. At this, Michael became offended and determined to leave home. He shipped as a cabin-boy on a vessel called "The Maryland Merchant;" his brother followed him on board the ship and on his knees begged him to give up this rash intention, but to no purpose. He had set his face toward America, the wonderful new world and from this course he was not to be turned. He landed in America in the year of 1767, and was apprenticed by the captain of the boat to Robert Craton of Virginia. He remained there until the outbreak of the Revolutionary War when he enlisted and served under General George Washington, and was present at the surrender of Cornwallis. At the close of the war he immigrated to Kentucky and located at Strodes Station in Clark County. From there he moved to Fleming County and established what afterwards became known as Cassidy's Station. For ten years endeavoring to hold his home and hearth-stone, his life was one continuous struggle with the blood-thirsty savage and the stubborn wilderness. His personal appearance was peculiar, being very low of stature, measuring barely five feet, and yet heavy enough to weigh one hundred and seventy pounds. To describe Michael Cassidy more fluently, it could be said that he was built with strong, short legs, he was barrel-chested, with thick, strong arms and large hands with almost unbelievable strength, his shoulders were broad and strong and supported a short, thick neck. His face and head gave the appearance that he was chiseled from a solid piece of granite. Michael Cassidy was not a mold, he was a type all by himself that was never duplicated in appearance, shrewdness and bravery. For his daring feats in Fleming County and this part of Kentucky, he stood alone.

There are many amusing stories connected with his "smallness." Upon one occasion, his camp was surprised by the Indians and his two companions, Bennett and Spor, were killed; Cassidy was overpowered and captured. His captors thinking that he was a boy turned him over to the smallest of their party to be butchered for their entertainment, but the victim did not propose to be led like a lamb to the slaughter, and so vigorous and persistent was the conflict that the two Indians were compelled to assist in clubing the boy to the ground. In falling, Cassidy's hand fell upon one of the Indian's knives, and rising to his feet, he flourished it with such ferocity that the Indian gave back and Cassidy darted like a deer into the deep woods and made his escape. He carried to his grave the marks of this terrible conflict.

Upon another occasion, while a member of the Legislature, he was addressing the House, when the chairman seeing his head just above the shoulders of those seated near him, cried out, "Is the gentleman from Fleming County sitting or standing?" Tip-toeing to his greatest height, Cassidy roared back, "Standing, Sir, with my full height which is less than six feet."

The grave of Stuart, the spy, who was killed by Cassidy is still to be seen on the farm that was known as the William Robertson farm. This was to Cassidy the most regretful act of his life, although he was in no way to be blamed for it, and Stuart before he died, completely exonerated him from blame in the matter. Stuart, it seems, was employed by the whites as a scout whose duty it was to keep them posted to the movements of the Indians, thus he usually dressed in the guise of the Indian. It was understood among the whites that no gun was to be fired in hearing of the Station except at a "Redskin." One evening, when approaching the settlement, he was tempted into shooting a large owl. Cassidy seized his gun and started in the direction of the shooting. Stuart getting sight of him took refuge behind a low-forked tree and raising his head up between the forks to make himself known was shot through the forehead by Cassidy.

Michael Cassidy was one of the most noted men of the brave pioneers and Indian fighters whose exploits gave to Kentucky the name "Dark and Bloody Ground." More than thirty years were his close and deadly conflicts with the Indians. Brave, resolute and watchful, he was well-fitted for his task and mission, and neither was the one left undone or the other a failure.

We, who are sitting today in perfect safety in our warm and modern homes with plenty stored away for the coming winter, riding in ease and pleasure over concrete roads in our cozy car at a speed that is almost unbelievable, little realize or appreciate the hardships, dangers and privations of that sturdy band of men and women who made these things possible. It is a good idea that by these sketches they should once more stand before us in their rugged and undaunted courage.

Michael Cassidy seems to have enjoyed the confidence of the people of his community, having filled many positions of honor and trust. In 1797-98, before Fleming County was formed, he represented Mason County in the lower House of Kentucky Representatives. On the forming of Fleming County out of part of Mason, he became her first Senator in 1800-06, in 1808-09-17-20-22 we find him representing Fleming County in the Lower House. He was one of the Judges of the first court of Quarter-session.

Michael Cassidy died March 19, 1829, having been a member of the Presbyterian Church for thirty years and was buried at Old Brick Union with the honors of War. In his coffin was laid away one of the most noted men connected with the history of Fleming County. His descendants are numerous and well-known to most of our citizens.

The Brick Union Cemetery is located three miles east

of Flemingsburg, Kentucky on State Highways 111 and 32. It contains one acre of ground and was cut from the farm known as the Farris farm. This cemetery for years had grown up into such a wilderness that, undoubtedly, hundreds of interested people passed there every day not knowing that it held the remains of Michael Cassidy and other prominent men of this part of Kentucky.

About forty years ago, Rev. J. J. Dickey of Flemingsburg, a retired minister, although feeble with old age at the time, took it upon himself to clean this cemetery in which he did a splendid job. But not long after this fine job was done, Rev. Dickey, passed on to his reward and in a few years the cemetery had grown up into its former state. The Campbell Brothers, Cliff and Clyde, who were progressive business men of Flemingsburg and Fleming County, again had this noted cemetery cleared of its filth (at their own expense), and to look at it from the highway as one passed, you could almost say that it was beautiful. The cemetery now (1971) is again in a bad state and the author of this book hopes to see this old and famous cemetery again cleared and enshrined as a landmark to Fleming County and to the brave pioneers, both men and women, who have found their last resting place within its boundary.

It is not known to this writer to whom or when Michael Cassidy married, but Samuel E. Cassidy, his son and his wife, Elizabeth A., lived in Flemingsburg and were the parents of two sons, Roger and his brother, Gilbar A., who was one of Flemingsburg's most noted attorneys.

Roger Cassidy, son of Samuel and Elizabeth A. Cassidy, was born on the 29th day of March, 1865, on the old Cassidy homestead near Flemingsburg. (The Cassidy home was a large two-story brick home at the edge of town). This home burned to the ground in the early 1930's. A nice modern frame house has replaced the brick home and it, with the farm, is the home of Mr. and Mrs. Joe Simons.

Roger Cassidy was the grandson of Michael Cassidy, one of the pioneer settlers of Fleming County. He was reared on his father's farm until the time of the latter's death in

1882, after which he remained on the farm until he was 24 years old, when he came to Flemingsburg and engaged in the livery business. He first formed a partnership with Jesse W. Lee under the firm name of Lee & Cassidy, then he purchased Mr. Lee's interest and continued in his own name for some time. Later, he formed a partnership with Charles Lee, which he continued until September, 1895, when Jesse W. Lee purchased Charles Lee's interest and the business was conducted under the style and firm name of Cassidy and Lee, and so continued for a number of years.

Roger was married on the 3rd day of March, 1887 to Miss Alice Evans Hawley, and to this union was born one child, Harry Cassidy, who has made a famous name for himself, and you will read more about him at the last of this chapter.

Having sprung from old pioneer stock who braved the danger, hardship and privations incident of the early settlement of Fleming County and the foundations of future wealth and prosperity, Roger Cassidy inherited those stern qualities which gave force and energy to business and industrial enterprize. In its day, the firm of Cassidy and Lee built a prosperous business. In every sense they went a long way, and were prepared with every facility for rendering every satisfaction to the public, where they invited attention to their stock and outfit in general.

HARRY CASSIDY

Detective of the Famous Lindberg Kidnaping Case

Harry Cassidy was one of the hand-writing experts in the kidnaping-murder trial of Bruno Richard Hauptmann, who was tried and convicted for the kidnaping and murder of the nineteen-month-old son of Col. Charles and Anne Morrow Lindberg at their home in Hopewell, New Jersey. The trial opened January 2, 1935. The jury retired to study the evidence at 11:23 a.m. on February 13, 1935. At 1:44 p.m., the jury entered the court room and announced: "We, the jury, find the defendant, Bruno Richard Hauptmann, guilty of murder in the first degree." And on April 3, still vigorously maintaining his innocence, Hauptmann paid the penalty of death in the electric chair for the murder of the Lindberg baby.

Harry Cassidy was born and reared in Flemingsburg. His father, Roger Cassidy, was city marshal of Flemingsburg for a number of years. He was the grandson of Samuel Cassidy and the great-grandson of Michael, who was one of Fleming County's pioneer settlers and Indian hunters.

The remains of Michael Cassidy and his family were moved from the Brick Union Cemetery in the early 1930's to a prominent lot in the Flemingsburg cemetery with appropriate markers.

CHAPTER THREE

THE FORMING OF FLEMING COUNTY

This paragraph has some interesting facts of how Fleming County was formed. From a copy of an old newspaper that has no name of the paper or the editor on it, but starts out this way: "The first act of organizing the County of Fleming approved Feb. 10, 1798. Be it enacted by the General Assembly that from and after the first day of March, 1798 all that part of county of Mason included within the following bounds, to wit; run a line south from the Court house of Mason County to the north fork of Licking River, thence up the north fork nine miles when reduced to a straight line to the mouth of the Flat Fork of Johnston, thence to the mouth of Fleming, a straight line, down Fleming to the mouth, and up Licking to the head thereof, and with the line of Montgomery County to the Virginia line, thence with the said line to that branch of Sandy which divides this state from Virginia, thence down the said branch till it intersects a line drawn from the beginning as follows, to wit: from the upper north fork to the head of the south fork thereof, thence with the dividing ridge between the waters of Licking and the Ohio, until it strikes the water of Sandy, then down such branch east to Sandy, to be called and known by the name of Fleming.

"After the said division takes place, the courts of the county of Fleming shall be held on the second Monday of every month and the courts of quarterly session shall be held annually in the months of March, May, August, and November in such manner that is provided by law in respect of other counties within the state.

"Section 3. The justices named in the commission of the Peace for the said county of Fleming shall meet at the house of John Faris in Flemingsburg, in the county of Fleming, on the first court day after the said division shall take place, and having taken the oath of office prescribed by law and sheriff being duly qualified, the court shall proceed to appoint and qualify their clerk and fix a place for their seat of justice for the said county, and proceed to erect the public buildings at such place for the permanent seat of justice, and a clerk be appointed (except pro tempore) unless a majority of the justices of the court for which the clerk be appointed.

"Section 4. It shall be lawful for the sheriff of the county of Mason to make distress for any public dues or officers fees, unpaid by the inhabitants of Fleming County.

"Section 5. The courts of Mason County shall jurisdiction in all action and suits depending at the time of said division.

"Secton 6. Until an enumeration be made, agreeable to the constitution the said county of Fleming shall be entitled to one representative in the General Assembly, and the said County of Mason shall retain the remaining three. This act shall commence, and be in force from, and after the first day of March, 1798 . . ."

CHAPTER FOUR

SALATHIAL FITCH

Salathial Fitch was born in the State of Maryland, Oct. 1, 1764. He migrated to Kentucky with his wife and one child in the year of 1788. The conveyance used by him in the great part of his long and tedious journey was a sled; but on reaching the Ohio River, passage was procured for the rest of the way in a flat boat. Landing at Limestone, now Maysville, late in the month of May, a temporary home was found in one of the neighboring forts. The season was so far advanced that other emigrants, who came at the same time, thought it not advisable to attempt making a crop; but Mr. Fitch determined to try the experiment. Accordingly, on the 27th of May, he began to clear away the forest, with his wife piling the brush, and on the 27th of June, he planted two acres of corn and pumpkins. The soil being rich and fresh, these two acres yielded an abundant supply for the family. About the year of 1794, Mr. Fitch settled in the unbroken forest, three miles north of where the town of Flemingsburg now stands, and continued to reside there until his death.

In the year of 1810, having been recommended by a majority of the Magistrates of the county, he was commissioned by the State as a Justice of the Peace of Fleming County. This office he held until the year of 1826, when as the Senior Magistrate of the county, he according to the law as then existed, became High Sheriff. Having executed the required bond as Sheriff, Mr. Fitch — as was the custom of the law in those days — sold the office and John Stockton became the purchaser.

Although the subject of this sketch was a decided member of the old Whig party, acting and voting with it from earnest convictions that it was right, he was also a true patriot. In the War of 1812, he was past the age to perform the duties of a soldier, but his eldest son, Henry, went into the Army and was a member of Captain Botts' Company.

Mr. Fitch had joined the Methodist church in his native state of Maryland and as soon as he was settled in his western home, he sought to avail himself of the religious privileges afforded by the denomination of his early choice. With this in view, he gave the ground and was instrumental in building a church where Fitch's Chapel stood for a number of years. This was one of the first Methodist churches built in Fleming County. Mr. Fitch was for many years a steward in his church and beneath his roof the pioneer preachers ever found a cordial welcome. Among those who partook of his hospitality, we mention the name of Bishop McKendree.

Mr. Fitch was the father of eleven children, all of whom, but one, lived until they were grown; and his son, John, occupied the old Fitch homeplace for many years. Mr. Fitch was a man of good judgment and of sound integrity, and as an officer, whether in the church or state, he was faithful to his duties. He died in 1842, having been a good man and useful citizen, and having left his moral impression upon his family and upon the neighborhood in which he lived.

CHAPTER FIVE

OLD FLEMING COUNTY RECORDS

Proceedings of the First Court Ever Held in Fleming County, Kentucky
(Taken from a newspaper account)

This will be interesting to many people, some of whom are doubtless descendants of the parties composing the first court that was ever held in Fleming County in 1798. "Agreeable to an act of the General Assembly of Kentucky, entitled an act of the Commonwealth and from under the proper hand of his Excellency James Garrard, Esquire, Governor of the State of Kentucky, bearing this date the twelfth day of February, in the year one thousand seven hundred and ninety eight was produced, directed to Richard Tilton, George Ruddell, Andrew Kincaid, William Kennan, James Harris, John O'Hara, James Henderson and Adam Brevard, gentlemen of the County of Fleming, therein constituting and appointing the aforesaid gentlemen Justices of the Peace with powers in and for said county of Fleming, whereupon George Ruddell, Esquire, administered the oaths required by law to be taken and the oath to support the Federal Constitution to Richard Tilton, Esquire and said Richard Tilton, Esquire administered the said oaths to the aforesaid George Ruddell, Andrew Kincaid, William Kennan, James Henderson and Adam Brevard, Esquires.

"At a court began and held for Fleming County at the house of John Farris in the town of Flemingsburg on the ninth day of April in the year of our Lord one thousand seven hundred and ninety eight and in the six year of the Commonwealth. Present:
Richard Tilton, George Ruddell, Andrew Kincaid, William Kennan and Adam Brevard, Gentlemen Justices.

"Ordered that Joshua Stockton be appointed clerk of the court pro tempore. Whereupon the said Joshua Stockton took the oath to support the constitution of State and United States and also the oath of office and together with George Stockton Sen., his security entered into an acknowledged bond in the penalty of one thousand pounds conditioned for the true and faithful performance of his office—.

"On the motion of Joshua Stockton, Thomas Scott was appointed Deputy Clerk who took the oaths to support the constitution of the State and United States and also the oath of office.

"John Keith, gentleman, having produced a commission under a seal of the Commonwealth appointed him sheriff of the County until the next general election who thereupon took the several oaths prescribed by law to be taken and together with George Stockton, sen. and Michael Cassidy his sureties entered into and acknowledged bond in the penalty of three thousand dollars conditioned as the law directs.

"Ordered that the court be adjoined to the house of William Robinson. These minutes were signed Richard Tilton. At a court continued and held for Fleming County present Richard Tilton, George Ruddell, William Kennan, James Henderson and Adam Brevard, Gentlemen Justices.

"Andrew Kincaid, gentleman, having produced a commission under the seal of the Commonwealth appointing him surveyor of Fleming County until the end of the next session of the General Assembly took the oaths prescribed by law to be taken together with George Stockton, Sen., and John Hart his securities entered into and acknowledged bond in the penalty of five hundred pounds conditioned as the law directs—.

"An indenture of bargin and sale from Edward Wilson and his wife, Jane, to James Inlows was proven by the oaths of Michael Cassidy, Josiah Richards and John Howe witness thereto and ordered to be recorded—.
Present, Andrew Kincaid, gentlemen Justice—.

"It is decreed and ordered by the court that the members of the court who are now present meet at this place on Saturday before the next court of quarter sessions held

34

for the county in order to receive propositions and to view and fix upon the most convenient place for erecting the public buildings on—.

"The court being dissatisfied with the penalty of the bond which Andrew Kincaid has given for the performance of his office as surveyor of this county, George Stockton, Sen., came into the court and undertook for the said Andrew Kincaid that in case the bond which was already given was deficient that at the next court he would give bond in such penalty as the court should direct—.

"Joseph Curry and Ira Kneeland are appointed to examine such persons as Andrew Kincaid shall recommend as Deputy Surveyors for this county who thereupon took the oath prescribed by law—.

"Mahalabeel Shakle having produced credentials of his ordination and also of his being in communion with the Methodist Episcopal Church, a testimonial is granted him for celebrating the rites of matrimony between any two persons to regular applying therefore he having made oath and entered into acknowledged bond as the law directs.

"Ordered that the court be adjourned till tomorrow at ten o'clock. These minutes were signed: 'At a court for Fleming County the tenth day of April, 1798, and sixth year of the Commonwealth.'

Present: Richard Tilton, Andrew Kincaid, and William Kennan, Gentlemen Justices.

"Ordered that a writ of ad quod damnun issue directed to the sheriff of Fleming County commanding him that by the oath of twelve honest men of this bailwick he view the bed on both sides of Fleming Creek where William Secrets is desirous of building a water grist mill, and to assess the damages, if any, which the said Secrets or any other person may sustain by erecting the said mill and make report to the next court and is further ordered that this order be complied with on the last Friday in this month—.

"Ordered that Thomas Jones, John Hart, Robert Morrison and John Threkeld or any three of them being first sworn to view the old ways leading from Hugh Fultons to the Upper Blue Licks and report to the next court which way they conceive to be the best with such amendments as they think necessary together with the conveniences and inconveniences attending opening the same—.

Present: George Ruddell, Gentleman Justice—.

"Ordered that Francis Baker, John Jones, Cornelius Gooding and Jasper Seybold or any three of them being first sworn, to view from the junction of the Salt Lick and Three Islands Road, Glascock's nearest and best road from thence to Flemingsburg and report to the next order court the conveniences and inconveniences attending opening the same—.

Absent: William Kennan, Gentleman Justice—.

"On the order of William Kennan ordered that suit of ad quod damnun issue directly to the sheriff of Fleming County commanding him that by the oaths of twelve honest men of his bailwick he view the bed both sides of Fleming Creek, where William Keenan is desirous of building a water grist mill and assess the damages, if any, which the said Kennan or any other person may sustain the said mill and it further ordered that this order be complied with on the _____ William Kennan and Adam Brevard, Gentlemen Justices—.

"Ordered that Thomas Brown and Samuel Hart be appointed commissioners to take in the taxable property for the ensuing year who made oaths according to law—.

"Michael Cassidy's stock mark a slit in each ear. On motion of George Stockton, junr., ordered that a writ of ad quod damnun issue direct to the sheriff of this county commanding him that by the oaths of twelve honest men of his bailwick he view the bed of both sides of Stockton Run where the said Stockton is desirous of building a water grist mill and to assess the damages, if any, which the said Stockton or any other person may sustain in erecting the said mill and it further ordered that this order be complied with on the eleventh day of this month—.

"On motion of William Robinson it is ordered that license be granted him to keep an ordinary at his house

36

in this county for one year, he having given bond with Alexander Simpson as his security conditioned as the law directs—.

Absent: Richard Tilton, Gentleman Justice—.

"Richard Tilton, having produced credentials of his ordination and communion with the Methodist Episcopal Church a testimonial is granted him for celebrating the rites of marriages between any persons to him regularly applying therefor who made oath and executed and acknowledged bond as the law directs.

George Stockton, junr., Stock mark a crop and a slit in each ear.

Present: Richard Tilton, Gentleman Justice—.

Ira Keenland and Bryam Rout having produced a certificate of the qualifications as Deputy Surveyors of this county took the oaths prescribed by law.

Present: James Henderson, Gentleman Justice—.

"On the motion of Robert Gray he is exempted from paying county levies. — Ordered that Richard Tilton, William Kennan and John Howe be appointed commissioners to take depositions to perpetuate testimony on the entry made by Benjamin Roberts on Fleming—.

"Thomas C. Lawson's stock mark two under bits out of the right ear — Hugh Fulton, James McIntyre and John Hart or any two of them are appointed by the court as commissioners for the division of lands in the county between residents and non-residents—.

"Ordered that the sheriff of the county let out to the lowest bidder the erection of stocks in this town and that they be erected by the May court, and likewise a stray pen which is to be made of good rails, forty feet square with strong bars, ten rails high and locked—.

Richard Tilton and Andrew Kincaid are appointed as judges on the on-suing election and William Keenan, clerk.

"Ordered that a county seat be provided for this county and that Joshua Stockton be appointed to transact with a workman for the same with this devise to be made thereon "United." —

Pursuant to law the court doth settle and rate the following prices of liquors, diets, lodgings, provender pastures, and stablage at and for which the several ordinary keepers in the county are to sell for the ensuing year "to wit."

	Shilling	Pence
For warm dinner _____	1	6
For warm breakfast or supper with tea or coffee _____	1	3
For cold meals _____	1	0
Whisky per half pint _____		6
Whisky bounce per half pint _____		9
Whisky rum per half pint _____	2	0
Wine per bottle or quart _____	9	0
Cider per quart _____		9
Bedding with clean sheets _____		6
Stabling pr. 24 hours or night _____	1	3
Horse to hay 12 hrs. in day _____		6
Oats per quart _____		2
Corn per quart _____		2
For pasture 24 hours _____		6

Elisha Adamson, William Newcomb and Patrick Shannon being appointed as constables of this county came into the court and took the oaths prescribed by law to be taken and entered into and acknowledged bond as the law directs.

"Ordered that court be adjourned till court in course." These minutes were signed Richard Tilton.

CHAPTER SIX

JOHN COCHRAN

John Cochran made history in what is now Fleming County, Kentucky, but when he was born in 1784 in Ireland, Fleming County had not then been carved from Mason, nor Mason from Bourbon for that matter. His father emigrated to this country when John was very young and settled on Hinkston Creek in Bourbon County, Kentucky. After the elder Cochran and family had settled their home and cleared about four or five acres of ground to grow enough food to survive the coming winter and year, John was put in the hands of a Mr. Green as an apprentice to learn the carpenter and cabinet trade, earning a small amount of money which was paid to his father, plus his board. John and the Greens got along well, especially when Mr. Green would occasionally take him on a day's hunting trip to replenish their larder with wild turkey, grouse, squirrel, deer and one time a black bear. Mrs. Green treated John as one of her family. The Green's home and shop was known as the half-way house between Lexington and Paris. It was in this manner that John Cochran learned to be one of the best cabinet makers and carpenters in the years to come.

After serving his apprenticeship and completing his training, he was yet in his teens. However, he courted a Miss Mary Wasson and they were married on the 28th day of May, 1808 and the same year moved to Fleming County and located in Flemingsburg. Here he lived out a long and useful life with the exception of a few years that he lived in Tilton.

John Cochran was married twice and reared two sets of children. By his first wife, nee Wasson, he had five children, two sons and three daughters. They were James W., John C., Sarah, Minerva, and Eliza. His second wife, nee Cooper, had two children, Clement and Sallie. His second wife, after the death of her husband, married a Mr. I. K. VanSant. John Cochran came to this county when it was a vast wilderness, he literally grew up with it. He was a remarkable man for his generation and through a long and useful life he was one of the most influential citizens in the county. He and Samuel Stockton and James Eckles have left their mark on most every building in Flemingsburg built previous to 1850. John Cochran was an uneducated person but in life he was determined to succeed, always truthful and honest, and anything deceitful was foreign to his belief. He always ran his business on the cash system, he made no accounts and kept no books, yet he amassed quite a fortune for his day which he gave to his children and grandchildren a good portion of it in his old days, and left a good size estate when he passed away on April 1, 1863. He was buried in the old Methodist graveyard near Flemingsburg.

You could no more write a history of Fleming County and leave John Cochran out of it than to write a book without a title. Naming a few of the buildings that he built or helped to build in a span of over fifty years are: the first he built was the old Independent Bank Building of Flemingsburg which stood on the east corner of the public square and was owned by David Willson. The bank was at that time kept in the corner room, while the Willson's lived in the other portion of the house; he built the house of N. S. Andrews and a large house in which Mrs. I. K. VanSant lived and in which she died; also Methodist Church which stood on the lot where Alfred McDonald's residence was; he did the woodwork for the handsome brick residence of Dennis Belt and also that of Isaac Darnall where Wm. Quaintance lived later. He was called on to design many houses and did the woodwork on many more. The old market house which stood in the center of the street between the Exchange Bank and the Morris property, long since torn down, was built by Mr. Cochran and was for a long time one of the most noted institutions in town. In years past it was the scene of many election brawls and excitements. At that time an election lasted over a period of three days and the voters of the entire county came to Flemingsburg to vote. More will be written later about these fantastic three-day elections where they made speeches, sang, danced, cussed and discussed with fistcuffs all mixed in with their vote. All of this took place at the famous old Market House.

Mr. Cochran was also the only undertaker of Flemingsburg for nearly a quarter of a century. In 1833, 1849 and through 1855 when the cholera epidemic was raging in town and people were afraid to go out to minister to the sick or to bury the dead, Mr. Cochran met the occasion that he was called upon to do, and was of invaluable service in burying the dead. Mr. Cochran was Whig in politics, although he never sought any office, nor would he accept any nomination to office or an appointment. When the Whig party disbanded, he acted with the Democrats, and when the Civil War broke out he was a strong Union man and took a very decided stand that way. He joined the Home Guard Company and helped guard Flemingsburg against invasion. At the time the war broke out he was the owner of many slaves of which he freed at a great loss.

Mr. Cochran's son, Clement, died young. All the rest of them grew to be useful men or women. His sons, James W. and John C. were long-time residents of Lexington where they owned and operated the firm of J. W. & J. C. Cochran Dry Goods. It was one of the largest businesses of its kind in Central Kentucky. The firm has long since dissolved. James W. was later engaged in the insurance business and filled many public offices, serving many years as treasurer of the city and councilman and director of the Northern Bank. John C., after leaving the dry goods business, was sheriff of Fayette County. When the war broke out, he was commissioned a Colonel of the 14th Kentucky Infantry. Daughter, Sarah, married James C. Newcomb, but died a few years later; the second daughter, Minerva, married Hiram T. Pearce of Maysville; the third daughter, Eliza, married Elias B. Pearce of Poplar Plains; Sallie married M. A. Weedon of Flemingsburg. The writer of this article has had the pleasure of knowing some of the subject's descendants, but acquired a good bit of information from records and newspaper clippings.

CHAPTER SEVEN

JOSEPH PORTER

Biographical sketch of Joseph Porter, who was born two years before George Washington became President of the United States.

Joseph Porter was born at Red Stone Old Fort of the Susquehanna River in the state of Pennsylvania on February 10, 1787, according to an old newspaper clipping with no name of the paper or editor, identified only in this way, Number XVII, by M. O. The article states that Joseph Porter's father, who was Joseph P., Sr. was born in Ireland in 1758 and came to Fleming County in the year of 1806, when he was nineteen years old. He resided on the waters of Three Mile Creek in Fleming County, a small stream that empties into the Licking River, about midway between Tilton and Sherburne. He had lived there ever since he first came to Fleming County which this article states was seventy years ago. Some years ago the writer, who identifies himself only as M.O., with elder Hawkins of Tilton paid the old gentleman a visit. The article states that they found him in fair health for one so far advanced in age. He was almost blind, could only tell night from day, but his mental faculties were remarkably good; his recollection of his boyhood to them was good.

After shaking hands with him and giving him their names, though he was acquainted with them did not recognize their voices, he inquired if they had come especially just to see him. On being told that they had, he seemed pleased and entered into a very interesting conversation. He gave a brief history of his life from childhood down to the present, interspersing it with pleasing antidotes of early times, giving dates as readily, and doubtlessly as accurately as many historians of the present day. As he sat there in his easy chair by the fireside, his cheeks and brow furrowed by the passing of many winters and summers, his lengthened locks white as the driven snow, gave one the feeling that he was talking to a person who was almost as famous as Santa Claus. There he was, surrounded by his children and his grandchildren, he stamped a deep picture in one's mind that time will never erase of one who is contented and happy. The elder Porter having heard much of the fertility of the soil in Kentucky — and he always was a tiller of the soil — decided to make that territory his future home. So in company with another family, likewise immigrating to the west, he came down the Ohio River in a flat boat built by himself for the purpose of landing at Limestone, which is now Maysville in the month of April, 1789, before George Washington was inaugurated President of the United States, and three years before Kentucky became a state. Joseph Porter, Jr., the subject of this sketch, was then only two years old.

From Maysville, Porter and his family were transported by wagon to Paris, the only town between the two points was at the Lower Blue Licks. The country as a whole was almost an unbroken wilderness, with lurking savages still to contend with, who were hunting for your scalp or your horses. A guard accompanied the wagon all the way, but in due time they arrived at their destination without any trouble. Paris at that time was a sparsely populated town. Shortly after Mr. Porter came to Kentucky, the Virginia legislature made Paris the county seat of Bourbon County, under the name of Hopewell. The Porters settled on what was called military land on Hinkston Creek, six miles from Paris. This land was owned by John McDowell, a grand uncle of Dr. Lucien McDowell of Flemingsburg. After living there thirteen years, he moved to the adjoining county of Fayette, living on the land of Hon. John Breckinridge, grandfather of General John C. Breckinridge. Here he remained until New Year's Day in 1806, when he moved to Fleming County upon the farm that now is owned by Joseph Porter, Jr., where in 1810 Joseph Porter, Sr., died. In numerical order, he was the twelfth child in a family of thirteen — five sons and eight daughters — of whom he was the only

44

one living at the time this article was written.

When he immigrated to the west, Kentucky was a part of Virginia and was composed of nine counties: Bourbon, Woodford, Fayette, Mercer, Madison, Jefferson, Nelson, Lincoln, and Mason. Three years later it became an independent state. Lexington was established as its capitol and Col. Issac Shelby was chosen first Governor. The schools then were few and far between. Mr. Porter tells us that he started to school at the age of seven and went for only a few years. In the year of 1813, he married Miss Mary Dillion of Fleming County, and shortly afterward began housekeeping on the farm that he then occupied. He reared a family of ten children, eight sons and two daughters, all of whom at the time of the interview were still living, seven in the state and two in the state of Missouri. Three sons, Will, Doc, and Frank, never married and lived a long and useful life, died and were buried on the farm on a beautiful hillside just a short distance from the residence. The Porter farm is still in the Porter family. Mr. "Johnny Buck" Porter, their nephew, next owned the farm and lived to a ripe old age. Several years before he passed away, he had the Porter graveyard on the farm put in perfect condition, with a concrete wall about four feet tall and about one foot thick built around it, with no gate, the only entrance is over the wall. At "Johnny Buck's" death it passed on to his son, David D. Porter, who repaired the buildings, cleared the land, built roads, ponds and fences. At his death it fell into the hands of his wife, Mrs. Ivetta Peck Porter and their only child, Mary Frances, who is the wife of Dr. John Robert Cummings, a noted doctor in Cincinnati, Ohio. They have two children, Mary Wallace and David Porter Cummings.

CHAPTER EIGHT

THE BOTTS OF FLEMING COUNTY

To write any history of Fleming County, Kentucky and its oldest and most prominent citizens, it would be an injustice to the state and county to omit the name of Botts, who have been connected with the county of Fleming soon after, or perhaps before, it was formed.

The subject of this sketch, William Scott Botts, was born in Flemingsburg on the 18th day of February, 1810. His father was George Washington Botts of Stafford County, Virginia. He moved from that state to Fleming County very early in its history and married Ann Scott of Fayette County, Kentucky, by whom he had two children, William Scott and George A., of whom the subject of this sketch was the elder by fourteen months. Having lost his mother when only seventeen months old, his training and education devolved upon his father whose careful attention to the development and training of his son compensated in great measure for the irreparable loss at so early an age of a mother's tender care.

When six or seven years old he was put in school and continued a regular attendant in schools taught in Flemingsburg by various teachers until the spring of 1825, when he was sent to a select classical school in Fayette County, Kentucky taught by Rev. Robert Marshall. The following winter, he returned home and enjoyed the instruction of the Rev. James Birch who had opened a classical school for boys in Flemingsburg the preceding autumn. In the spring of 1826 he returned to Fayette County and attended a classical school three miles from Lexington taught by the Erudite George Clarke. In October, 1826, he entered the Sophomore class of Transylvania University, where he remained until the autumn of 1827 when the fame of the University of Virginia attracted him, with many of the ingenious youths of the state to its classic halls. He remained at this seat of learning until the fall of 1829 when he commenced the study of the law near Danville, Kentucky with the late Chief Justice Boyle and attended the lectures of that eminent Jurist in Transylvania University during the session of 1829-30. Continuing his studies with Judge Boyle during vacation, he completed his second of lectures at the Department of Transylvania in March, 1831 and obtained a diploma.

In February, 1831, more than a month previous to his graduation, he obtained his license to practice law from the Court of Appeals, which then had upon its bench Justices George Robertson, Joseph R. Underwood and Richard Buckner. Possessed with an ample income, he was not forced upon the completion of his course of legal study to the practice of his profession, and the following year he attended a post graduate course of law at Transylvania, returning to Fleming County in 1832 where he resided, devoting the larger part of his time to the study of history and Bell's Letters, both of which departments of learning he was exceedingly fond. From his return to his native hearth in 1832 until November 18, 1842, the agreeable task of entertaining himself and friends was the most difficult one that fortune saw fit to place before him. The loss of his fortune in 1842, necessitated his application to the practice of his profession upon which he entered in November, 1842, when he took the room over the (then) Exchange Bank which were rendered familiar to many citizens of the county by his occupancy.

Mr. Botts was elected to the Legislature in 1841 and again in 1846. He found in the practice of his profession and duties at Frankfort an abundant occupation of his time and energies. Upon the adpotion of the Constitution of Kentucky in 1850, he was elected Judge of the Fleming County Court and upon this retirement from that office in 1854, he resumed the practice of his profession which he prosecuted without intermission until 1862 when he took his seat a third time as a member of the Kentucky Legislature, which position he retained until his elevation to the

State Senate in 1863. As a member of that body, he was appointed Chairman of the Finance Committee, which responsible position he held during his incumbency and discharged its delicate and responsible duties with honor and credit to himself and the Senate. Returning to private life in 1867, upon his expiration of his term of office he steadily pursued — the even tenor of his way occupying a large part of his time in professional work. Though he did not hold a public office after 1867 his professional brethren of various bars of the then 14th Judicial District repeatedly elected him Special Judge in the absence of the regular incumbent.

As a lawyer, Judge Botts was accurate and profound, slow and cautious in forming an opinion, but tenacious of his position when once taken. In his favorite department of equity, he was met with deserved success, especially in the Appellate Court of Kentucky, where his careful preparation and clear, logical argument of equity causes had given him a degree of success hardly equalled by that of any other member of the profession in his District. By a careful and diligent attention to his practice, his uniform courtesy and unquestioned integrity, he succeeded in accumulating a handsome fortune and won the confidence and respect of his fellow citizens.

In his private career, he bore the burdens of state without flinching and discharged the duties of every office he ever held in a manner eminently satisfactory to his constituents. As a private citizen he endeared himself to many friends by his unostentatious but cordial hospitality, and by a prudent and careful observance of the laws of health preserved unimpaired a naturally vigorous and robust constitution.

In later years Judge Botts almost entirely withdrew from the practice of law finding his private business sufficient to keep him moderately busy and he lived a quiet and pleasant bachelor's life. At the age of sixty-seven, he was still hearty and robust and in the possession of his matured powers. The flame of life was still strong with an abundance

48

of oil to sustain it, and he continued to serve the State for several years.

CHAPTER NINE

THE OVERLEYS OF FLEMING COUNTY

John Overley, the father of Jacob Overley was born in the northwestern part of Virginia in what is now the state of West Virginia, about the year of 1761. His father, Peter Overley was a Dutchman — one of those hardy, adventurous frontiersmen who cultivated the soil, hunted the bear and the deer and fought the savage Indians. The son grew up to manhood in his father's home, was thoroughly educated in the use of the rifle, the axe and the plow, but had little knowledge of books. His parents spoke the German language and when twelve years old John could scarcely speak a word of English, but by the time he had doubled that age he had become sufficiently familiar with another language to make the daughter of a neighboring Welshman understand that he wished to marry her. So John Overley and Ann Jackson were married. John was born and reared amdist the stirring scenes of border life. He was becoming dissatisfied with his native home, the Frontier had receded, game had become scarce, the country was becoming densely populated and the young man had determined to seek a new home beyond the mountains where the fertile fields would furnish him bread and the forest furnish him meat. He had heard of the fertile fields and the abundance of game far away in Kentucky, so he prepared himself the best that he could and started on his long, hard and lonesome journey to the new life that awaited him in his adopted land.

He settled at Fleming's Station in what is now Fleming County, Kentucky in the year of 1790 or 91. This Station was owned by Colonel John Fleming, who had settled it just a short time before. It was two miles north from the town of Tilton, about five miles south of Flemingsburg and one mile north of Martha Mills. The Garr Pond graveyard was not far from where the Fort stood and where the settlers buried their dead, it is yet to be seen. Fleming Station was built upon a little knoll, at the base of which is a fine spring. This furnished water for the use of the settlers, except during periods of very dry weather when it had to be carried from a larger spring several hundred yards distance. This spring is situated in a little cove on the hillside fronting Fleming Creek and nearly opposite to what was the James P. Bell farm.

Just over from the spring, and commanding a good view of its surroundings, is an elevated point of land. John Overley used to say that he always crept cautiously to the brow of this hill, and looked over to see that no lurking Indians were near to shoot him with an arrow, before venturing to the spring for water.

About the year of 1793, the Indians made their last excursion into Fleming County, stealing some horses from settlers near Fleming's Station. The whites raised a party and pursued the marauders, John being one of the company, but the Redskins made good their escape with the horses, crossing the Ohio River at the mouth of Cabin Creek, six miles above Maysville, Kentucky (then known as Limestone).

John Overley bought a tract of land about two miles west of Fleming's Station and built a house on it, into which he moved his family about the year of 1795. Here he spent the remainder of his life — more than half a century — dying in 1854, at the ripe old age of ninety-three years old. He raised a family of ten children — eight sons and two daughters.

Jacob, the subject of this sketch, was born in the year of 1802, being in numerical order, the seventh child. The boys were all raised on the farm and taught the laborious occupation of tilling the soil, which in return yielded them bread. Thus developing and strengthening their physical powers upon which they were to depend for a livelihood in after years. The land was to be cleared and fenced, roads were to be opened, the crops were to be planted, cultivated and harvested and many other kinds of hard labor performed, all without the aid of machinery such as the present day affords. When not engaged upon their father's farm, the boys assisted their neighbors in clearing land, building, fencing or any other frontier work, so that all were constantly and profitably employed. There were no idlers in John Overley's family — all had to work. Children were not so expensive a luxury in those days as they are now and the cost of supporting a family was then trifling in comparison with what it is at present. Most of the food was produced upon the farm and obtained from the forest, wool from the sheep was then made by hand into jeans and linsey to supply both sex with winter wear, while course linen made from flax raised on the farm constituted material for summer clothing. Children from infancy to ten or twelve years of age, usually wore but a single garment, a "slip" which was nothing more than a long shirt made of linsey or linen. The father generally made the shoes (there were no boots in this part of the country in those days) of leather tanned by himself. A few of the settlers could make hats, these supplied the demand for that necessary article, though coon-skin caps were then quite fashionable. Just let the reader imagine a party of a dozen or so young ladies and gentlemen of the present day clad after the fashion of their grandparents — the ladies with coarse, homemade shoes, buckskin gloves, a linsey-woolsey dress and hood of the same material; the gentlemen in leather breeches, coonskin cap and linsey hunting shirt — and he has the picture of a family of young girls and boys in their Sunday best.

During Jacob Overley's pupil age, the country afforded few schools and those were of an inferior grade, so that his opportunities for acquiring a good education was quite limited. He attended several winter schools, learning to read, write and cipher as far as the teachers themselves could go, after which by close application to books in his leisure hours at home, he gained a general knowledge of men and matters. For forty years before his death he was never known to be without a newspaper and for that reason was always well posted in the current events of the day.

52

At the age of twenty-two he married Mary, daughter of Frederic Beckner of Fleming County and aunt of William M. Beckner, who was later editor of a Clark County newspaper. Mr. Beckner then owned and occupied a farm two miles west of the town of Sherburne, Kentucky. This farm was later known as the John Peck farm. Shortly after his marriage, he began housekeeping on a tract of land belonging to his father on the north side of Fleming Creek one mile from Martha Mills, being a portion of the farm that was later known as the N. H. Crain farm. Being strong and hardy, he labored assiduously for several years clearing, planting, plowing, harvesting, but fortune being unkind to him, he at length became dissatisfied with his home here and determined to seek a change of life in some more favored locality. He had heard much of the cheapness and fertility of Indiana's soil, and so determined to make that state his future home. In the spring of 1832 he landed at the town of Rising Sun, Dearborn County, (now Ohio County). He did not buy land, but rented as much as he desired, and at once proceeded to test the quality of Indiana's soil. He found it no more productive than what he had left in Kentucky, while many advantages he had enjoyed in his Kentucky home was wanting in his home in Indiana. A residence of two years in that state seemed to have satisfied him. In the fall of 1834, found him snugly settled on a little farm in Bath County, Kentucky, not far from the town of Bethel. Here he remained for eight years — longer than at any other place since his marriage. In 1842 he bought and moved to the old Jacob Chrisman farm in Fleming County adjoining the one upon which he had begun life for himself eighteen years before.

Jacob Overley's wife had been an invalid for a good many years, which for several years she was confined to her bed. Her protracted illness was a serious drawback to the husband's prosperity, as much of his earnings was expended in vain endeavors to restore her to good health.

Early in life Jacob confessed his Saviour, connecting himself with the congregation of christians at Log Union

Church. This was one of the first houses erected in Fleming County for the purpose of religious worship. This church has long since been gone and no one living today can remember it nor can the site where it once stood be located. It was also known as the "Old Dunker Church." It's pulpit was for thirty years occupied by Rev. Peter Hon, a Dutch minister of the gospel, who in his more youthful days had belonged to that peculiar sect called "Dunkers." Now all of the congregation have long since passed away, only the oldest citizens that are living today can remember their parents and grandparents of days gone by speaking of this old church and the graveyard that was near by. The general direction where this old church stood is known, but I know of no mark that would indicate the spot. Although in his second childhood, the good old pastor, Peter Hon, would have reached his one hundredth birthday if he had lived only a few more months.

In politics Jacob Overley was a Whig and adhered to his party with great tenacity as long as it survived. He was a great admirer of George D. Prentice and for many years a constant reader of his paper, (The Louisville Journal), the editor being one of the most prominent leaders of the Whig party in Kentucky. In May 1851 with his associate, Abram Gooding, he was elected Justice of the Peace in the Flemingsburg district, the first under the new constitution. Again in 1855 he was elected to the same office in the Tilton district, having previously changed his residence to that precinct. Archibald Hull (Democrat) was chosen with him. He was elected in 1859, this time in company with Elijah Thomas, serving in all twelve years as a Justice of the Peace for Fleming County. Squire Overley's legal attaniments were necessarily limited, but he possessed and exercised excellent judgment and dispensed his old-fashion, off-hand justice with such scrupulous impartiality that few of his decisions were ever reversed by higher courts. Jacob Overley raised a family of six children, three sons and three daughters. During the Civil War he remained a staunch adherent to the Union. His sons, however, divided; two of

54

them, Thomas and Pinckney becoming soldiers in the Union Army, the other, Milford, with a single companion made his way through the Union lines to the south, where he enlisted in the Confederate Army. Once during the war, Pickney and his Rebel brother were engaged in the same battle, though at the time neither was aware of the presence of the other. This division upon the part of the sons was the source of much anxiety to the good old father, but to increase his trouble, in 1863 his son, Thomas, who was a member of the 10th Kentucky Cavalry was desperately wounded in an engagement with Scott's Louisiana Cavalry C.S.A. in Estill County, Kentucky. While the war was progressing, Fleming County was frequently visited by roving bands of armed men professing to be Confederate soldiers but who were not recognized as such by the War Department at Richmond, and who, in reality, were nothing more or less than robbers.

Their sole object was plunder and they cared little in what manner or from whom they obtained it. On one occasion the subject of this sketch was arrested upon the highway by a party of these marauders from Morgan County and robbed of his horse, saddle and watch. His stables had previously been visited under cover of darkness and a valuable mare taken by those engaged in the "Secret Service." When the War ended, the kind heart of Squire Overley was made glad by the safe return of his soldier boys. They all met at the parental home, both Union and Confederate, where they were received with expressions of glad welcome, but the former were not more cordially and affectionately greeted by the patriotic father than was he who had espoused the Rebel cause and fought under the Rebel Banner. All cast aside party prejudice and each accorded to the others sincerity and honesty in their political views and the same freedom of thought and action which he himself had exercised in the troubles just ended. The manifestation of this spirit of liberty toward one another by all the members of the family, and especially by those recently in open hostility and still differing so widely in their political sentiments, was the means of re-establishing and perpetuating feeling that should exist among those so closely connected by the ties of consanguinity. No reconstruction laws were necessary in that household — kindness and charity accomplished what their opposites could never have done — reunited in sincerity and truth a divided family.

Jacob Overley was now an old man with but few years intervening between him and the grave. The cares of life and the weight of years had whitened his head and shattered his once vigorous constitution. She with whom he had shared life's joys and sorrows still lingered in affliction and was his comfort and care. Tenderly, kindly had he nursed her through the long, weary years of her sickness and till death had ended her suffering. Jacob Overley outlived his wife but a few months, and now he reposes by her side at the old Log Union Graveyard that has been almost forgotten, and probably lost forever to all but God.

MILFORD OVERLEY
The Son of Jacob Overley, Who Honors the Chapter Above

Milford Overley was of Scotch-Irish and Dutch-Welsh descent. He was born in Rising Sun, Indiana, December 23, 1834 during a temporary residence of his parents who were natives of Fleming County, Kentucky, but who had taken up residence in the Hoosier state for about two years. Milford was raised on a farm in Fleming County, attending the public schools and working during vacation time. By applying his book knowledge to his everyday life, he acquired a good education for those days. For some years preceding the Civil War, he taught school in Bath and Nicholas Counties. In 1856 he was married to Miss Mary E. Hughes, a young lady of fifteen years of age. Five years later with a single companion, he made his way through the Federal lines to Virginia, where he enlisted in the Confederate army. Upon being transferred to the command of General John Hunt Morgan, he received a commission in the 9th Kentucky Regiment; later when General Morgan was captured, he then served under General Joe Wheeler till the close of the war.

56

Surrendering as one of President Davis' escort on the 10th day of May, 1865, he fought in Kentucky, Tennessee, Virginia, South Carolina, and North Carolina, participating in nearly fifty battles in all, yet he came out without a scratch. At the end of the war, he returned home and resumed teaching, which he followed for several years. Later, he was elected Superintendent of Schools for Fleming County which position he held for eight years, then he was examiner of teachers for Fleming County for twenty years. Again he became engaged in farming until his little granddaughter was left an orphan; then he moved to Flemingsburg where he raised and educated her.

CHAPTER TEN

WILLIAM QUAINTANCE OF FLEMING COUNTY

The subject of this sketch was born in Rappahannock County, Virginia, December 7, 1785. In company with his family, he came to Kentucky in 1795. The family consisted of father, mother, two older brothers and two sisters. His father was an English sailor who settled in the Jerseys. His father bought and improved a farm about four miles north of Flemingsburg that was later known as the Jonathan Lewman farm of Mt. Carmel. Here William Quanitance spent the days of his youth farming. When the War of 1812 broke out, he enlisted in Captain Belt's Company and was attached to Colonel Pogues' Regiment and spent the winter of 1814 in the northern part of Ohio.

After his services in the army, he returned home and was soon afterwards married to Miss Sabry Southard of this county. To this union was born four sons and four daughters. Soon after his marriage, he bought and improved a farm about midway between Flemingsburg and Mt. Carmel. (This farm was later known as the Josha DeBell farm). On this farm he built a mill and distiller and manufactured flour, meal and whiskey. He took a great pride in his mill and always claimed that he made the sweetest meal, finest flour and purest whiskey in the state. Notwithstanding, he was a manufacturer of whiskey, he was an ardent temperance man, having been a member of the first Temperance Society ever organized in Fleming County.

In June of 1833 he lost his wife by the cholera epidemic of that year. During the prevalence of this fatal disease he went about visiting the sick and buring the dead. It was some time that year that he sent for the preacher in charge of the Methodist Church and requested him to enroll his name as a member on the church book, claiming that he had been a member all of his life, having been baptized in infancy and having observed the ordinances of the church for many years. He was enrolled a member and ever afterwards lived a true and consistent Christian.

In politics, he was always a Whig but never a politician. He voted for the Whigs because he believed in Whig principles. He never held office nor was he ever a candidate. At the outbreak of the Civil War, his whole heart and soul was enlisted in the Union cause, but before it lasted long he became utterly disgusted with the position he had taken and abandoned it. He cast his last vote for President for General McClellan, the Democratic candidate for president in 1864.

His son, William S., was one of the best and most substantial citizens. He was engaged in farming and stock raising. Aside from his agricultural pursuits, he took a lively interest in public affairs and was one of the most generous friends to the public enterprise and welfare to be found anywhere. He concocted a plan for securing substantial and economical insurance against fire, and mainly through his efforts, the Farmers' Home Mutual Insurance Company of Fleming County was organized and put in successful operation. He resided a few miles from Flemingsburg on the Elizaville Road.

About the beginning of the Civil War he sold his farm and bought a house and lot in Flemingsburg in which he lived until his death, which occurred January 7, 1867, at the ripe old age of eighty-two years.

CHAPTER ELEVEN

PROMINENT CITIZENS OF FLEMING COUNTY
Who Were Born and Lived in the Early 1800's and 1900's

MR. WILLIAM S. FANT

The subject of this sketch was one of the most promi-ent enterprising business men of his native county where the scene of his life was laid. He was born near Hillsboro, Fleming County, Kentucky on the farm now owned (1971) by Mr. Ogden O. Story. Mr. Fant was born on the 21st day of May, 1830, and was the youngest child of the family of two sisters and one brother. His parents, Nelson Fant and Mary (nee White) Fant emmigrated from Stafford County, Virginia in the year of 1813. Mr. Fant enjoyed only such advantages as were afforded him for an education as the neighborhood school at the time afforded him. When he was eleven years of age his parents located at Poplar Plains in Fleming County, which was then denominated as "The Hub" of the county as to wealth and influence. Here he attended school as favor-able opportunity offered and ran the picking machine in the carding factory of his father until in 1847 he moved with his father to the farm. Subsequently, he left the farm and went with his brother-in-law, Silueius Garfield, who had purchased the carding factory and flouring mill at Sherburne in his na-tive Fleming County. Mr. Garfield was conspicuously known in northeastern Kentucky as a superb business man, politi-cian, editor, orator, legislator and judge, having been elected as a delegate to the Constitutional Convention of 1850 by a Democratic majority of 250. He was afterwards a delegate to the Constitutional Convention of California and contribut-ed largely to the framing of the state constitution of that state, returning to Kentucky and assuming the editorial con-trol of a Democratic paper at Paris, Kentucky. He was elected as a delegate for the state at large in the presiden-tial campaign of 1856, after which he was appointed by the President, James Buchanan, as Judge of the United States Court for Washington Territory.

The retirement of Mr. Garfield from business at Sherburne forced Mr. Fant to take entire charge of the mill at the age of twenty, where he remained in active business until June, 1869, when he moved to Flemingsburg, the seat of Fleming County. In 1872 he purchased the flouring mills at Flemingsburg, then a burr mill. In 1886 he changed it to a roller mill, and continued to put in the latest and most valuable modern improvements until it was one of the best mills in this part of the state. In December, 1868, he added to his business by a purchase of the Pleasant Valley Mills and 1898 the Nepton Mills; in each of which he placed valuable improvements.

Mr. Fant also invested largely in real estate, owning farms in the states of Texas and Indiana in addition to his holdings in Fleming County which was over 1,000 acres, and a tract of 425 acres in adjoining Bath County. He was the owner of about forty dwellings and business houses in Flemingsburg which he built himself. He also owned the controlling interest in the capital invested in the then Deposit Bank of Pearce, Fant & Co., (now The Farmers Deposit Bank) of which he was president. Mr. Fant was one of the county's best business men of his day, from a strictly business point of view, that the county ever had. Born of parents of limited means, he carved his way to a successful career by his own energy. He dealt with all mankind with the motto of "Live and let live"; no worthy appeals were heeded with a deaf ear and the appeals of charity were never turned away empty. As a faithful and consistent member of the Christian Church and elder of the same since 1857, he at all times contributed liberally to every effort made to the advancement of the cause and was chiefly instrumental in the erection of the beautiful and artistic building in Flemingsburg in which the Christian denomination meet for worship. He also was a member of the Masonic Fraternity which, no doubt, greatly impressed him with the responsibilities and duties he owed to mankind. The lives of such men are a blessing, and their virtues and example worthy of the imitation of generations to come.

CHAPTER TWELVE

TAKEN FROM "THE FLAG" (EXTRA)
Flemingsburg, Kentucky, September 28, 1847

"We issue an 'Extra' this morning on the occasion of the anticipated departure of the Flemingsburg Volunteers, that the public may know the names of the brave men who go to fight the battles of their country.—

While this 'extra' is issuing from the press, the Fleming Volunteers are partaking of a dinner, prepared for them by the citizens of this place. They will leave for Maysville tomorrow.

FLEMING VOLUNTEERS

The following list comprises the names of the brave boys, who constitute the company under command of Capt. Cox who will march from this place tomorrow, to the place of General Rendesvous:

Capt. Leander M. Cox
1st Lt. William T. Walker
2nd Lt. John M. Headleson
3rd Lt. Marshall L. How

Non Commissioned Officers

1st Sergeant, James L. Crain
2nd Sergeant, Elias Markwell
3rd Sergeant, Samuel Sweet
4th Sergeant, John B. Rock
1st Corporal, John F. Jones
2nd Corporal, John Wood
3rd Corporal, John Donaldson
4th Corporal, John M. Evans
Fifer, Henry B. Dudley
Drummer, James B. Cassidy

Privates

Alexander Andrews
James W. Achison
Amb T. Alender
James D. Alender
Charles Arnold
William Beckner
Alfred C. Berry
John Balls
Edward Barnaby
John S. Bradley
Robert W. Bradley
Josiah H. Cord
Wm. A. Crain
Wm. P. Cox
Wm. Collins
Wm. P. Clary
John D. Combess
Alfred Clary
Hiram P. Crain
James Cary
Edward Cary
Thos Coale
Simon P. Carpenter
Alfred Cline
Saul F. Cline
Andrew Chrismine
Darius Dixon
Daul Dalrymole
John T. Farris
Jesse Falls
Jefferson Foundray
Washn Foudray
Andrew Glass
Milton Goodwin
Saml Gorman
Irvin Gilkison
Thos F. Harper

Jno. P. J. Helvestine
Saml Hawes
J. M. Henderson
H. C. Helvestine
Roland Hedrick
Saml Ham
Wm. H. Jones
Wilson F. Kirk
Fer'and Kirkham
Wm. Kissick
Walter J. Lacy
John Lawson
Robert G. Lewis
Avery G. Littleton
Nicholas Litton
Wm. Moss
Geo. W. Markwell
Geo. W. McIntyre
Elijah Mahan
James McCracken
James L. Nealis
Wm. B. Obannon
Wm. O. Pepper
John J. Porter
John M. Pearce
Jackson Roe
Jacob Rice
Daniel Runyon
Wm. Ringo
John R. Ricketts
Thomas L. Ringo
James D. Ringo
H. Clay Stockton
Richard Schennk
Geo. W. Sevain
John T. Sumerall
Robert Shanklin

64

Nicholas Sutton
Greenberry Traylor
John P. Umstattd
Eli C. Wilson
Joseph Williams
Marcus Wise
Alfred F. Graham
Dillard Zimmerman
Henry B. Asbury
John T. Grose
Moses W. Coleman
St. Clair Emmons
James Nealis
G. W. Vanlandingham
Wm. W. Bridges
Alvin Markwell

Joseph Clark
Parker V. Prater
Robert Ringo
Wm. Welch
Calvin Moore
Wm. Kelly
Thomas Swim
H. Linthicum
Mordecai Wells
James McGraw
John Crozier
Wm. Sullivan
Edward McLaughlin
Monroe Philips
Elijah Reed
David McCord

16TH KY. VOL. INFANTRY U.S.A.

Flemingsburg was host to the fourth annual re-union of the 16th Kentucky Volunteer Infantry and those who survived the Battle of Franklin, Tenn. Capt. M. C. Hutchins of Maysville, President, presided and Comrade Jos. I. Dorsey was called to the secretary's chair. The following veterans answered the roll call:

Company A

Elias Young, Ewing
Geo. Berz, Mayslick
C. Paul, Maysville

J. T. Robb, Sardis
P. Walton, Wash'on
J. Burns, Oakwoods

Company B

E. W. Bell, Johnson
S. P. Gully, Wallingford
W. Ferin, Wallingford
Geo. Ross, Wallingford
E. H. Jones, Sandford

Jas. Hurst, Wallingford
W. A. Gooding, Wallnfd.
J. Hammond, Sandford
W. K. Ham, Sandford
J. E. Hurst, Sandford

G. McDonald, Carlisle

Company C

T. A. Tearum, Okl.   W. B. Dawson, Maysville
W. Chisholm, Mayslick

Company D

O. Bongham, Johnsville C. Little, Lonoxburg

Company E

G. Clinger, Maysville   Wm. Cox, Augusta
B. Weaver, Augusta   A. Martin, Millersburg

Company G

W. Steele, Wedonia

Company H

T. J. Wood, Tilton   J. L. Overley, Tilton
R. S. Finley, Tilton   W. B. Scott, Bethel
J. Cogar, Mayslick   T. W. Coaper, Nepton
L. W. Hess, Illinois   W. F. Hendrick, Flem'rg
J. I. Dorsey, Flem'rg   J. P. Dorsey, Flem'rg
J. P. Hendrick, Flem'rg C. L. Overley, Maysville
J. L. Dorsey, Flem'rg   H. W. Hall, Carlisle

C. L. Overley was elected President; L. W. Hess, Historian; G. M. Clinger, Secretary; T. J. Wood, Treasurer; Rev. J. P. Hendrick, Chaplin. After dinner, Jno. P. McCartney gave the welcome address and Capt. M. C. Hutchins responded. Chaplain Hendrick introduced Elder Wm. Stanley who was a gallant aide on the staff of Gen. Jno. B. Hood C.S.A. Augusta was selected as the place of meeting."

CHAPTER THIRTEEN

JUDGE R. H. STANTON

This article was taken from a clipping of a newspaper which is not named concerning the meeting of the Circuit Court in Fleming County, Kentucky, on Aug. 14, 1873, which at that time was composed of Mason, Fleming and probably one or two more counties.

"The August term of Circuit Court commenced its sitting in this place on last Monday, Judge R. H. Stanton, presiding; George T. Halbert, commonwealth's attorney; the following gentlemen compose the grand jury: Thos. R. Botts, P. M. Samuel, A. P. Hord, Jno. H. Fields, Thomas F. Keerans, N. G. Little, Wm. H. Cord, W. B. Cord, J. B. Jackson, Andrew Hedrick, W. B. Obannon, Johnson Ross, Wm. Rice, Holman Hedrick, John Bell and A. B. VanSant. The petit jury was as follows: Issac Vanarsdall, Samuel Hiner, B. E. Davis, J. B. Jones, Eli Plank, W. H. Smith, Thomas P. Sutton, Chas. Nute, G. A. Henderson, Resse Davis, B. A. Glascock, Jno. Crain, H. C. Berry, Geo. M. Caywood, Samuel Blair, H. P. Jones, Jerry Story, E. A. Robertson, Jno. Peck, Robert D. Howe, Dr. J. C. Waugh, Milford Overley, Jas. W. Hull, Jno. S. Darnall. Among the lawyers that attended from a distance upon the court, we noticed the following: Hon. E. C. Phister, Maysville; W. B. Prather, Cynthiana; Taylor Young, Morehead. Some of the trials that were disposed of at that court were as follows: Elijah Purcell was fined 100 dollars for carrying concealed weapons; Westly Berry for keeping a tippling house was fined $50; Skaggs for standing a horse without license was fined $10; James Lee indicted for horse stealing was sent to the penitentiary for four years; Alford Shackleford indicted for petty larceny was sentenced to receive ten stripes; Sep. Owens for larceny to receive seven stripes.

"On dismissal of the Grand jury of that term of court of which the Hon. Judge was not too well pleased with what was done, or rather with what was not done, he made the statement that there were more pistols in the county of Fleming than there were plows and cows, and that in the future, he hoped that the grand jury would find out more about what their job consisted of and act accordingly."

The first light shown on the life of this great man started in the far off state of Washington in the city of Walla Walla, when a patriotic club there knew that their state was named for our first President, but was curious to know by whom and why it was so named. Their secretary, Henry Kelling, wrote to the Courier Journal in the city of Louisville, Ky., and his son gave this information:

"Richard Stanton was born at Alexandria, Va. Sept. 12, 1812, and was a descendant of John Stanton, who came to Virginia from London prior to 1626. His father's name was Richard Stanton and his mother was Harriet Perry (or Petit) of Huguenot extraction. He was educated in the private school of Benjamin Hallowell, a famous Quaker teacher of that day. In 1833 he married Asenath Throop of Fairfax County, Va. and came to Kentucky and settled at Maysville, Oct. 10, 1834. This place became his permanent home and remained such until he died, Oct. 1891. He entered active life as a lawyer and editor, having established The Maysville Monitor, the first Democratic paper published in Northeastern Kentucky, about the year 1835, and continued as its editor through the presidential campaigns of 1840 and 1844. After that, he was appointed Postmaster at Maysville and held the office until he was elected to Congress in 1849. He served three terms in that body and was defeated for a fourth term by Hon. Leander M. Cox, who was the nominee of the Native American or Know-Nothing Party of that day.

"After his service in Congress, he resumed the practice of law successfully and continued it until the breaking out of the Civil War, when he was arrested as a Southern sympathizer by General William Nelson and taken with several other Kentuckians as political prisoners to Camp Chase. He afterwards was removed to Fort Lafayette, outside New York harbor, where he remained until near the close of the war, when he was released by the personal order of Mr. Lincoln, who did not require him to take the 'ironclad oath' which he had so long declined to take as the price of his enlargement. At the close of the war, he again resumed the practice of the law and began the preparation of the large series of law books, the publication of which distinguished him as a law writer.

"In 1868 he was a candidate for the Democratic nomination for Governor, but was defeated by Gov. Helm. He declined the nomination for Lieutenant Gov., and Hon. John W. Stevenson was nominated in his place. Gov. Helm died immediately upon assuming the office and Lt. Gov. Stevenson succeeded to the Executive Chair, immediately following this, Judge Stanton was elected Circuit Judge of his district and continued as such for several terms, when he was defeated by Thomas F. Hargis, who afterward became Judge of the Court of Appeals. Judge Stanton then resumed his practice and the compilation of his books.

"He compiled Stanton's Codes of Practice, Stanton's Statutes, Stanton's Digest, Stanton's Treatise, Stanton's Guide to Justice, Stanton's Guide to Executors and Administrators, and a number of other works which were generally used by the bar of the state. The legislature purchased a large number of his books for use among the officers of the state.

"While in Congress he was a very active and efficient man — a hard worker and the originator of a number of important measures. As Chairman of the Committee on Public Buildings and Grounds, he did much to adorn and beautify the city of Washington. The dome of the Capital is called 'Stanton's Monument.' He introduced the first bill for its erection and asked an initial appropriation of $50,000 which was laughed at as a monstrous extravagance, and it was only through the most strenuous effort that it was passed. At the succeeding session, he asked and obtained with difficulty another appropriation of $100,000, and the next term $500,000. The entire cost of the dome when completed exceeded $1,000,000 exclusive of the allegorical fresco on the ceiling of the dome, which alone cost $40,000.

"When the question of establishing the Territory of Columbia was before Congress, he moved to strike out the word Columbia and insert Washington, and to the adoption of this motion is due the name of the present state."

Judge Stanton was an imminently practical man in all of his public action as in his private life. He dealt little in theories that were not well adapted to practical use. His percepitons were excellent and his mind quick in action. As a judge his decisions were rarely overruled by the Superior Court and as a lawyer his cases were handled with marked ability.

After a life of high integrity and great usefulness, he died at near 80 years of age, generally respected throughout the state and deeply lamented by his friends and all who were near to him. His widow, past 80, survived him, as did three sons and four daughters.

* * *

Died, The Widow Of Judge R. H. Stanton

"The widow, of the late Judge R. H. Stanton is now laid at rest beside her famed husband, after three years of widowhood.

Mrs. Asenath T. Stanton, formerly of this city (Maysville), died Monday night at the home of her son at Carrollton, Ky. She was in her eighty-third year. She was born at Alexanderia, Va., in 1811, and came to Kentucky with her husband in 1834. The greater part of her life was spent in this city, where she was honored by all that knew her. She was a lady of exceptionally high moral and intellect force and produced a number of beautiful paintings in oil. Her husband, the distinguished jurist and congressman, preceded her to the grave three years ago. Seven children of Judge and Mrs. Stanton survive. They are Major Henry T. Stanton, Frankfort, Ky.; Richard H. Stanton, Jr., of Carrollton, Ky., in whose home his mother died; Clarence L. Stanton, Cincinnati, Ohio; Mrs. Trock Forman; Mrs. J. W. and Mrs. L. W. Pierce, Fern Bank, Ohio; and Mrs. W. E. Oakley, Crawford, New Jersey. The remains were brought here last night and after services at the Episcopal Church at 10 o'clock this morning, they were borne to the Maysville cemetery and laid beside that of her husband, who was one of Kentucky's outstanding citizens."

CHAPTER FOURTEEN

M. M. TEAGER,
ATTORNEY OF FLEMINGSBURG, KENTUCKY

Michael Moores Teager was born in Bath County, Kentucky, May 1, 1833. His father was of immediate German descent, a native of Lewis County, Kentucky, and a farmer by occupation. His mother, Louise Moores Teager was a native of Bath County, Kentucky, and was a daughter of Michael Moores, a veteran soldier of the Maryland line of the War of American Independence and of Sanai Harlan, a relative of Major Silas Harlan, who fell at the Battle of Blue Licks, and of the entire numerous family of Harlan's of Kentucky and other states of the Union.

Michael Teager was reared on a farm with his parents, who were of competent but ordinarily of limited means. Remote from the seat of learning, his education was the district schools of the day, with a short term at Antioch College, located in Ohio, in 1859. After teaching school about two years, he located in Flemingsburg, Kentucky, where he studied law, and in February 1860 he was admitted to the Bar. In October 1862, he enlisted in the Confederate army in Company B, Second Calvary in which service he continued until the termination of the War. After which, in May, 1865, he returned to Flemingsburg and resumed the legal profession. He enjoyed the confidence of his people by promotion to various official positions. He was appointed and served as Deputy County Clerk from 1866 to 1868, and as Deputy Circuit Clerk from 1868 to 1870, when he was elected County Clerk and re-elected in 1874, serving eight years. In 1880 he was elected County Prosecuting Attorney for a term of four years; at the expiration of which he was appointed Master of Chancery and served in that capacity until 1893, when he resigned to accept a position under appointment in the U. S. Internal Service, which he held until June 1,

1899 when he resigned, having served four years under President Cleveland's Administration and two years under that of President McKinley.

At an early age he developed a decided literary taste and inclination, and became a contributor of numerous letters and poetical articles to the newspapers of the day, which attracted the attention of the leading politicians of his Congressional District, who in 1858 tendered him as editor of a Democratic newspaper which he declined for reasons personal to himself. From 1870 to 1880 he was employed as assistant editor of The Flemingsburg Democrat, and was elected a member of the Kentucky Press Association by which he was appointed to the honor of preparing and delivering the annual poem of the Association at its annual meeting at Shelbyville, Kentucky, on June 3, 1875, for which he received many complimentary notices of the press.

At various intervals he wrote numerous poetical contributions to the Louisville Courier Journal and other papers and periodicals. Notwithstanding his active professional and official life, he resorted to literary study and pursuit more for pleasure and recreation than for personal reputation or profit. His productions all breathe a spirit of sympathy, charity and kindness, and a sentiment that thrusts upon the mind a refined sense of moral feeling and carries with them some lessons or maxim into moral and social life. His miscellaneous poems were carefully revised with a view to the possibility of their publication in book form at some future time. He later published a neat little volume entitled "Miriam," a story in blank verse and occasional rhyme, illustrating the influence of woman in her pious work of Christian charity and love. The work abounds with pathos, of fine poetical image, feeling and effect, and well deserves a place in every Christian home.

Mr. Teager was married on the 11th day of May, 1871 to Miss Irene Emma Stealey of Jeffersonville, Indiana, to whom three children were born — two daughters and one son.

CHAPTER FIFTEEN

THE RYANS FROM IRELAND TO FLEMINGSBURG, KY.

John M. Ryan was born in Clonwell, Tipperary County, Ireland on the north shore on the 26th day of January, 1848. He was married in the month of April, 1865 to Miss Mary Kating, daughter of James and Mary Hogan Kating of the same city. He came to America in the same year with his wife and were on board ship on their way when President Lincoln was shot. They landed in New York on the Wednesday following his assassination which occurred on the previous Friday. From there they went to Cincinnati, Ohio, where they remained for a few weeks. When in search of a better field for opportunities that might offer industry and enterprise, they left Cincinnati and came to Flemingsburg where they took up permanent location and resided there the remaining years of their lives.

To this union fourteen children were born. He pursued the occupation of a farmer for a number of years when his political aspirations urged him to enter the race for the office of jailer of Fleming County, in which he was defeated by William Christy of Hillsboro by a small majority. At the conclusion of Mr. Christy's term of office, he again become a candidate for the same office in which he was elected, and was also at the next succeeding term to succeed himself. After the expiration of his last term as Jailer, he served for many years as City Marshal of Flemingsburg. He also purchased what was known as the McDonald property, upon which he erected a hotel well adapted to the comfort and accomodations of the traveling and local public. Adjoining this property on East Water Street, he also purchased the property formerly belonging to M. A. Weedon of Mt. Sterling, Ky., upon which he erected a large brick building house (which at this date, 1971, is still known as the Ryan Building).

Mr. Ryan had been a man of business and by his energy

and enterprise valuable property was added to the city of Flemingsburg. While he devoted his attention to his official duty, Mr. Ryan had charge and management of the hotel and from which no one who sought refreshment at his table ever left it hungry.

It was said by many people that on Court Days, as well as other days, when some man would come in for an evening meal before going home, Mr. Ryan knowing the man's family and living conditions at home, would gather a large box of food and send it home to his family. The back door of this hotel was visited probably every day by some poor and hungry person and Mr. Ryan's wife, being equally as charitable as he, never turned any worthy person away hungry, regardless of their nationality or religion.

Of Mr. and Mrs. Ryan's fourteen children, I have only the record of one son, Mr. James H. Ryan, whose sketch will conclude this chapter.

JAMES H. RYAN

James H. Ryan was born in Flemingsburg, Kentucky on January 26, 1866, just eighteen years to the day after his father was born in Tipperary County, Ireland, and was the oldest son of John and Mary Kating Ryan. His education was chiefly acquired by the opportunities offered through the medium of the common schools taught in the city of Flemingsburg, which he attended at the usual intervals common to such schools until the year of 1887, when he at the age of twenty-one years, together with his father, opened a grocery and meat store in the Ryan Block on East Water Street in Flemingsburg which was owned by his father.

During the time that he was engaged in the grocery business, he was married on the 4th day of October, 1887, to Miss Mary McHugh, daughter of a well known and prominent farmer residing in the neighborhood of Flemingsburg. To this union four children were born.

After the misfortune of losing his business house and entire goods in a fire, Jim and Mary Ryan, being young and

75

with plenty of will-power, determined that any bad luck short of death or good health would not keep them down for long; so gathering together what they had left, they moved to a farm near Flemingsburg and engaged in the independent occupation of farming until 1893, when he was appointed by the prison Commissioner as a guard in the Frankfort, Ky. Reformatory, which position he held for a term of four years with credit to the administration and honor to himself. On returning to his home in Flemingsburg, Ky., he resumed the occupation of a farmer until 1899, when he opened a livery stable and feed business on Mt. Sterling Avenue, near the present location of the Flemingsburg Slaughter and Packing Company, where he gave close attention to stock left to his care and kept on hand first class livery outfits.

Mr. Ryan was a thorough business man, alive, active and progressive, losing not an hour that could be devoted to some profitable employment. The embodiment of honor, his word was his bond and all dealing with him was conducted upon his part on honest business principles, pursued with the same energy, attentions and foresight which placed him among the foremost business men of Flemingsburg and Fleming County.

(Note by the author of this sketch). Of the four children born to Mr. and Mrs. James Ryan, two sons and two daughters, only two are now living. The two sons when they were very young sought their fortune in the state of Texas, both becoming prominent citizens of that state as well as business men. The eldest of the daughters was Mae, who married Mr. Clarence Clary, who was of a well-known family of Fleming County; to Mr. and Mrs. Clary were born two daughters. The younger daughter, Gertrude, married Mr. Harry Conway. They had no children. Mr. Conway owned and operated a barber shop in Flemingsburg for over fifty years. He was probably one of the oldest barbers in years of service in the state. (I, the author, am also a barber, following the trade a number of years and in my younger days, before I had reached my majority, I worked for Mr. Conway for a number of years).

CHAPTER SIXTEEN

FLEMINGSBURG AND FLEMING COUNTY, KENTUCKY FROM 1828-1833

In March of 1836, the editor of the Times Democrat, published this very interesting letter from a former Fleming Countian. The editor starts out thus:

"We publish this week a very interesting letter from an old citizen of this place, David S. Danaldson, now living in Terra Haute, Indiana. It will be read with interest by all who feel an interest in local affairs. We shall be pleased to hear from Mr. Danaldson again at any time he may feel in a reminiscent mood, as he writes well. His letter will be found in our supplement.

Mr. Danaldson's letter as written: Editor of Times-Democrat: Some interesting reminiscenses of ye olden time.

Dr. Fleming has sent me a copy of your paper of February 19, which gives an interesting account of Flemingsburg of that date, which I have read with much pleasure, and which reminds me that perhaps something about your people of half a century ago might interest some of your readers. Living in your pleasant little city from 1828 to 1833, I have a vivid recollection of many of your prominent men of that date, both of the town and county.

The Flemingsburg Bar

The Flemingsburg lawyers of that day consisted of Major Wm. P. Fleming, Martin P. Marshall, Jas. Crawford, L. W. Andrews, Wm. S. Eckles, Jas. Jones, Wm. S. Botts and Thomas J. Evans. Major Fleming was an old land lawyer and arranged more land titles by compromise than by litigation, saving cost to clients and tedious suits at law. On court days he would come in from his farm house (La Grange) with a large satchel filled with papers and rest a while at his store room (Fleming & Danaldson) before proceeding to court where he did a large legal business, having one side of most every case.

Jas. Crawford and Wm. S. Eckles died early. Thomas J. Evans was an ardent Democratic politician of unsuccessful ambition.

One of the early speeches of L. W. Andrews, esq. was made before the Masonic Brotherhood at Andrew Todd's church on June 24, 1830. He appeared somewhat alarmed when he commenced but soon settled down, making an ex-cellent address, which received the thanks of the judge. Wm. R. Fleming and the writer hereof made the music on that occasion with two violins. Without drawing upon Mo-zart, Meyerbeer or Mendelson, we marched the procession up Water Street with "Bonaparte Crossing the Rhine" and back again with the strains of "Over the River to Charlie." These young professors of horse-hair and catgut were duly complimented in a horn.

Col. R. W. Thompson of Indiana served in Congress in 1841 with Mr. Andrews, and states that he was a useful member and well able to take care of himself and permitted no indignities, these two gentlemen are perhaps the only Western members of the Congress of 1841 now living.

The Physicians of Flemingsburg and Fleming County in 1828-1833

Dr. Dorsey, Dr. A. M. Huston, Dr. F. A. Andrews, Dr. Jas. W. Campbell, Dr. McDowell and Dr. Howe. Dr. Houston oc-casionally filled the Methodist pulpit as acceptably as he administered caloma and jalap. Dr. Andrews went thorugh the epidemic of 1832 like a young hero, as fearless as Nelson at Gibraltar or Wellington at Waterloo. He was worth his weight in gold, and though victims were falling all around him, he never abated his efforts or wearied in attention to the sick and dying. In those days it took iron nerves to keep people from flying to the woods, Dr. Andrews was adamant in this respect.

Flemingsburg's Local Merchants of 1828-1833

Thomas Wallace, Alexander & Stockton, Fleming & Danaldson, Jacob B. Early, Wm. Botts, Thomas Porter, and Jno. Triplett.

Jas. Alexander was a rare old gentleman, replete in anecdote and fond of a joke, and also a good merchant. J. D. Early removed to Indiana and became very wealthy. Mr. Wallace was a rich Irish gentleman and strict Presbyterian. Porter and Triplett were fine looking gentlemen, intelligent and prosperious merchants. Wm. R. Roper was Judge of the Circuit Court, an able jurist, and an excellent and impartial expounder of the law. Thomas Saffern was Postmaster being appointed by Andrew Jackson, who was at that time President of the United States. (Mr. Saffern's deputy was Mr. William A. Gorman). Gorman afterwards went through the Mexican War and in the late "Unpleasantness" southward, he commanded a Wisconsin Regiment, coming out a Brigadier General.

Robert Stockton was master of the Little Brick School House that stood on the neighboring hill. Joshua Stockton was clerk of the County Court and his son, George M., deputy. Leakin D. Stockton was clerk of the Circuit Court and Taylor Dudley, deputy. White swelling in early life compelled Mr. Leakin D. Stockton to use crutches.

The brick houses in those days were built by Jas. Eckles and the frame houses by John Cochran and Samuel Stockwell, Sr. Mr. Stockwell had two negro slaves, Jack and Jim, who were treated well by Mr. Stockwell. They were fine carpenters and were considered to be worth more in cash than any two slaves in the county.

The Cholera Epedimic of September, 1832
Decimated The Village

On its first appearance the doctors said "Be temperate and stand your ground." In a few days, however, they said "Take a bottle of brandy and hike to the woods." Fox Springs was then thronged with "Carpet Baggers." The first cholera case was a negro holster, occuring on a court day and some country people went to see him, among whom was Captain James Saunders, living eight miles from town towards the Upper Blue Licks, whose family consisted of fourteen persons. All died but one, and was buried by a squad from town, the neighbors refusing to appear. The whole country was terror-stricken, such was the violence of the disease. May it never return!

Other prominent men of Fleming Co. in the years of 1828-1833 were Jno. Andrews, who lived in the village of Sherburne and was a large trader in dry goods and produce from the Licking River to New Orleans, sending out flat boats every spring laden with flour, pork, lard, bacon, and many other things. James Andrews owned and operated the Martha Mills on Fleming Creek, successfully. (About three hundred feet of the dam that was built for this mill still stands, mostly rock, but a large portion of the earthen part of the rock dam still stands. There are rocks of smooth surface that measure from six by four feet, or larger, and are ten to twelve inches thick. This farm that holds this mill dam is thought to be a part of the original farm that Col. John Fleming owned, for which Fleming County was named. This farm is now owned by Mrs. Virginia Ellis Cooper, the wife of the author of this book).

Daniel Morgan went to the Legislature whenever he wished to do so. He was a fine violinist and at the huskings when the speaking was over, a fiddle was procured and his music brought down the boys by the score.

Mr. Noble Ficklen was considered to be the foremost farmer and landowner in the county. (He is buried at Poplar Plains, Fleming County, where he lived; he being the fourth great uncle of the author of this book). Other noted men of Fleming County were Henry Bruce, Dr. Lowry, Abram Gooding, Wm. Keenan, David Finley, George D. Sousley, Jno. and James Dudley who were prosperous farmers. Captain Jos. Belt, fond of fine horses and an admirer of Henry Clay, ran the hotel corner of Main Cross and Water Streets, the principal Inn in the city of Flemingsburg, in the years of

1828-1833." (It is now, 1971, the Farmers Deposit Bank).

Mr. Danaldson goes on and states that Flemingsburg was the sweet auburn of his early life, whose pleasant people he so well remembered, but he would now be a stranger in the home of his youth.

"Changes has written upon everything except my fond recollection of the friends I left in Flemingsburg in 1833. My parents rest in its soil beside their relatives, Wm. P. and Thomas W. Fleming. My early friends were the Faris', Andrews, and Stocktons, all having gone to the Happy Hunting Grounds beyond the Dark River. Its young men and amiable ladies of half a century ago still have an abiding place in my heart and memory; gladly would my feet press again its bluegrass pastures adjoining town, but in a re-visit to the place I . . ."

Author's note: This long and newsy letter of Mr. Danaldson's at this place is continued, but in all of my clippings, notes etc., I have no other information of this interesting man.

CHAPTER SEVENTEEN

A PROMINENT MAN OF FLEMING COUNTY WHO LIVED BEFORE AND AFTER 1900

E. M. MONEY

The Hon. E. M. Money was born on the 5th of June, 1845, three miles south of Tilton, Fleming County, Kentucky, and was reared on a farm and employed in the occupation of farming upon the old homestead (now, 1971, belonging to W. L. Ramey), until 1879. In the meantime in September 1864, he was married to Miss America Stewart. After 1879, he left the farm and embarked in the merchantile business at Sunset in Fleming County, in which he was continually engaged for ten years. After which, in 1890, he located at Battle Run in said County. His educational advantages were limited, confined entirely as such as he could acquire in the district common schools, consisting of the rudimentary branches of a plain, common English education as was taught in the schools in that day. His father, William Money, immigrated to Kentucky from the state of Maryland in the year 1820. His mother, Mary Duley, was born and reared in Mason County, Kentucky, near the town of Lewisburg. The opportunities offered to many others in the business and other affairs of life were denied him, being left entirely upon his own resources, with neither fortune or educational advantages, but being a man of strong practical mind with a will to buffet the waves of fortune and carve his own way through the bustle and turmoil of a busy world, he was successful in so far inspiring the confidence and esteem of those that knew him best, as to be entrusted in a representative capacity with their interests in the exciting turmoil which agitated our state if not the whole country. In 1899, Mr. Money was chosen by the Democrats of his county as their standard bearer in the contest for Representative from Fleming County in the Lower House of the State Legislature. Upon his nomination, he entered upon a canvass so active and vigorous that notwithstanding the heated bitterness that characterized the campaign, he succeeded in his election and promptly responded to his name and entered upon the discharge of his duty as a faithful and vigilant representative, and amidst the fury of the contest, assassination and military despotism, he was at all times found at his post of duty and ready to respond to his call upon the roll. Fearless and brave in his defense of the rights of the common people, "no threat or intimidation moved him from the path of his duty." With the record he held, he justly deserved the high respect of those he so faithfully and fearlessly represented. Mr. Money later moved to Hillsboro, Fleming County, and was from there elected County Judge of his county. He then moved to Flemingsburg, where he lived the remainder of his life, dying at a ripe old age.

CHAPTER EIGHTEEN

WILLIAM H. FISCHER
GROCER — WHOLESALE AND RETAIL

Among the business ventures, that of the grocery line is particularly conspicious. The old regime is materially changed as to accommodate the wants of the public in the character of goods placed upon the market. This is to a great extent due to the increased facilities offered in the matter of transportation and the method of furnishing canned goods, by which all varieties of fruits, vegetables, meats and other articles of popular and daily consumption are supplied with a readiness that furnishes each family in mid winter with the products of early spring and summer. Among the grocermen who answered these demands was William H. Fischer.

Mr. Fischer, a son of John G. and Mary Fischer of Germany, was born in Flemingsburg, Kentucky, December 25th, 1858. His education was entirely confined to that of the common schools of the time and such mercantile experience as he could acquire under the directions of his father. On October 10th, 1871, while in his 13th year, he opened a grocery store at a stand that he occupied until May, 1897, when he closed and settled up his business and made a trip to California, returning to Flemingsburg in December of the same year. He re-opened his store and operated it until his death in the 1930's.

Mr. Fischer's success was principally due to his industrious application and attention to the wants of the public in his line and his special adaptation to the line of business in which he had been reared and educated. In addition to these qualities, he had a strict regard for fair dealing in the best goods in his line combined with efforts to be promptly up to date with all the popular demands of the season, such as early vegetables from the earliest southern markets. Mr. Fischer deserved the reputation of being one of our foremost business men, self-made and dependent upon his personal efforts and business enterprise for his success. Honest, faithful and diligent, he enjoyed the patronage and support of an appreciative public. He bought his supplies in such large quantities from the wholesale houses which gave a large discount, so for that reason he was able to sell to other merchants in the county their merchandise at a discount which was hard to compete.

CHAPTER NINETEEN

DAN T. FISCHER,
JEWELER AND OPTICIAN

The energetic and enterprising subject of this sketch, Dan T. Fischer, was born in Flemingsburg, Kentucky in the year of 1865, and was the fourth son of John G. and Mary Fischer, who came from Germany to the United States and located in Flemingsburg in 1848. Dan T. Fischer enjoyed the facilities offered by the public schools of Flemingsburg for acquiring an education and at an early age evidenced a decided inclination to mechanism. While yet in school, he began the study of watch making, working after school hours, Saturday and during vacation. He made his first watch in 1879, when only fourteen years of age, having made every part of it except the dial. He made his first clock in 1881. In June of 1883, in addition to his jewelry work, he engaged in the sale of sewing machines, devoting two days in each week to repairing jewelry. In the winter of 1887-88, he went to Cincinnati and studied the art of engraving for the benefit of his own business. In January, 1897, he attended the Philadelphia College of Horology and Optics to perfect a knowledge of optics. In the same year, he went to New York and took another course in optics under the tutelage of L. I. Ferguson, President of the Optical Society of New York, and in September of the same year he finished his course in optics and received his diploma. While in Philadelphia he made a model of a watch of his own design on a large scale showing the scapement of a watch. In 1898, he opened a jewelry store of his own at the old stand of Jno. G. Fischer & Sons. In addition to his other work, he constructed an improved sewing machine entitled "The Fischer Sewing Machine" which he placed upon the market. There were but few men his age who displayed the activity, patience and perserverance to fit themselves for the active life as Mr. Fischer did. Relying almost entirely upon his own resources and his mechanical genius, he established himself as one who was thoroughly equipped for the various lines of business to which he devoted his time and energies. At an early age he fortified himself in the prosecution of a successful career.

Dan T. Fischer was one of the first men of Fleming County to see that concrete was the coming building material for the future. Mr. Fischer had a block of three business houses on Water Street in Flemingsburg, which in 1905, he razed and built one large and modern building. It was appropiately called "The Fischer Building" which still carries his name engraved in stone. After Mr. Fischer's death this building was purchased by Dr. J. F. Hall, a dentist, who operated a hotel and rented offices. A drug store, barber shop, Lerman's Dept. Store and the Post Office of Flemingsburg were in this building for several years, besides his own dental office. At Dr. Hall's death, this building was bought by his son, Dr. J. Lovell Hall, also a dentist. After several years, he sold the building to Jesse Paul Cooper, who is the manager of Lerman's Dept. Store, which now occupies the entire first floor.

CHAPTER TWENTY

JAMES P. HARBESON, CIRCUIT JUDGE
OF FLEMING COUNTY, KENTUCKY

This chapter will be in honor of several prominent men who have served with outstanding honor and devotion, not only to Fleming County, but to this section of Kentucky. Their names cannot be forgotten as long as there is a record. The first man to be so honored is the one who bears the name above.

Hon. James P. Harbeson was born on January 4, 1838 in Mason County, Kentucky, and was the son of Benjamin and Mary P. Harbeson, who were of Scotch-Irish descent. Judge Harbeson came with his parents to Flemingsburg in 1844. He was educated first at the Flemingsburg Seminary and afterwards, was three years under the tutelage of the Rev. James P. Hendrick at a special school. Subsequently, he entered a special school at Maysville, Kentucky in a class of twenty-five under the tutorship of Rev. Mr. Seeley, a Baptist Minister. After finishing his scholastic course, he went to Kansas in 1856. During the political troubles there, he was a participant in the embroglio of that memorable period — was at the sacking of Lawrence and the Battle of Ossawatomie against John Brown. In 1857, he returned to Fleming County, and in 1858, he graduated in law from the Law Department of the University of Louisville and commenced the practice of law in Flemingsburg, Ky. He continued his practice there until 1861 when he entered the United States Service in the Civil War as Captain of Company H. 16th Kentucky Infantry, Col. Charles M. Marshall commanding. He was later promoted to Major of the Regiment and served as such until the spring of 1863, when he resigned and entered into a partnership with Judge Thomas E. Marshall in the practice of law in the city of Louisville, where he remained until 1866, when Judge Marshall was appointed Judge of the Court of Appeals; then the subject of this sketch was appointed city Judge of Louisville. After the expiration of his city judgeship in 1874, he returned to Flemingsburg and soon after his return, his wife died, but he resumed the practice of law.

In 1882 and 1884 he was a prominent candidate for the Democratic nomination for Congress in the ninth Congressional District of Kentucky in which he was defeated by one vote in one race, and by only a fraction in the other. He was, subsequently, elected County Judge of Fleming County in 1890, and being nominated in 1892 for Circuit Judge, was elected to the office of Circuit Judge. At the expiration of his term, he was re-elected to that position which he held until his death.

Judge Harbeson proved to be an able and efficient Judge, a man of high sense of honor, true to the principles of right and justice, and unswerving in his legal opinion of what he believed to be right and just between man and man. Thoroughly conscientious in his views, both legal and otherwise, he never hesitated in expressing them in terms plain and unmistakable in that which he thought to be right.

In the case of Bracken County (in 1903), which sought to prevent the reading of the Bible and offering a prayer in public schools; Judge James P. Harbeson rendered the following decision: "The people of the state of Kentucky (not withstanding the flings that may be made at them) and the people of the United States are a Christian people. The Bible is not only the revealed will of God to man, prescribing man's duty to God and his fellow man from a religious point of view, but it is the basis of all moral ideas and of the principles upon which our National and State Government are founded. It is the view of the American people pre-eminently Catholic and of necessity above and beyond the reach of of sectarianism however properly that word may be applied to the various denominations and types of the Bible believers. This court cannot bring itself to believe that the Legislature of Kentucky in the Statue quoted, means the word sectarian in any other sense than denominational. If it had intended to prohibit the reading of the Bible in the public schools, it is inconceivable that it would not have said so in plain words that could not be misunderstood. The Bible is the foundation of the best and highest civilization of the world. Liberty and good citizenship are the outgrowth of its teachings always. No good book has ever been written, at least, since the dawn of modern civilization, that did not draw its best ideas and most elevated thoughts from the Bible. Millions of the money of the American people is spent every year in sending the Bible over the world and their opinion is great good has been thus accomplished. It is not possible that in the estimation of the Kentucky Legislature it is a sectarian book. Public policy forbids that such a construction should put upon the State 'As to the offering of prayer at the opening of the school to the God of the Universe, accepted by all Christian people as the Creator, Preserver and Benefactor of the human race,' we think it eminently proper and not in violation of the statue that it should be done in the prayers proved to have been offered there is neither sectarian nor denominational teaching. It is therefore adjudged that the plantiff's petition be and the same is hereby dismissed and that defendants recover of plaintiff their cost herein expended."

By Judge Harbeson's first wife there was born one son, James P. Harbeson, Jr., who was graduated from the United States Military Academy at West Point, as a Lieutenant in the States Army and served in the Philippine Islands during the war. He also served with honors in the Spanish War at Santiago and Puerto Rico.

His second marriage was to Miss Alice Andrews, daughter of Robert and Amy Andrews, by which there was born to him a large, interesting and intelligent family. Judge Harbeson at all times proved to be the soul of honor and a representative of true and honest manhood. Conscientious in all his relation in life and faithful to every trust reposed on him personally or officially, a gentleman from the old school, he had inherited many of the qualities that characterized the old Virginia stock, and was distinguished for gentlemanly courtesy and many qualities.

CHAPTER TWENTY-ONE

THIS SKETCH CONTAINS THE LIFE STORY OF CHARLES L. DUDLEY

Charles L. Dudley, son of Joseph and Harriet Dudley, was born in Flemingsburg, Ky., April 22nd, 1845. His early boyhood was spent with his parents until the outbreak of the Civil War. During the year of 1862, he enlisted as a Union soldier in the 10th Ky. U.S. Calvary. At the conclusion of the War he was engaged as a dry goods clerk in the house of Burnes, Rogers and VanSant. Not being satisfied with the four walls around him plus the roof above him that shut out the daylight from above, he quit his job and took up the carpenter trade at which he worked in the construction of a number of houses, superintending the building of all those lying on Cross Main Street, between the Railroad Depot to, and including the Bank Building that was occupied by the firm of Pearce, Fant & Co. (now housing the O. P. Kane Jewelry Co.). In the meantime he was the chief miller for W. S. Fant for several years. Leaving this position with Mr. Fant in 1882, he entered the firm of Atkinson & Co. as a partner. They were engaged in the hardware and implement business. In 1885, he disposed of his interest in this business to Mrs. E. H. Kenner. He then accepted a position with the McCormack Machine Co. as a salesman and expert mechanic, which he retained until he bought the stock of R. S. Hudson & Co. in 1893, at the present site which Mr. Dudley humorously called 7-cum-11 - 44 Street, where he carried on the agricultural implement business in all its branches for a number of years.

Mr. Dudley and his son, Roy, were connected with the agriculture and implement business, and for several years they carried in stock for the public at large — all kinds of farm implements, modern and new (for the day) wagons, buggies, carts, driving harness, saddles, wheel-borrows, fencing and a number of items that are too numerous to mention.

91

Beside the machine business, soon after the turn of the twentieth century, Mr. Dudley had the first Ford Agency in Fleming County, building a nice garage, with a large show room with basement equipped as a store and a first class mechanic repair shop. His business was then known as the Dudley Garage and Carriage Shop. His ads in the local papers were at times as amusing as he intended them to be; it would probably be as such "Look at the new Model T Fords of the 1916 Model, the very latest style, also buggies, saddles and horse collars, at Dudley Garage in Flemingsburg, Kentucky."

Mr. Dudley lived to be an old and useful man, dying in the early 1930's. He was first married December 2, 1869, to Miss Emma Franklin, who died June 12th, 1877. Three sons were born to this union, two of whom died in childhood and one, Franklin, who worked for a number of years between Cincinnati and Chattanooga for the Adams Express. He later retired. He was married the second time to Miss Lula Kenner, daughter of Leroy and Mary Kenner, May 5th, 1881. To this union was born three sons and one daughter. The sons were Roy, Woodson, and Bruce and the daughter, Carrie Douglas, a well known artist of New York. Woodson died when a young man; Roy died in a car accident in 1938; Bruce, a famous sports writer for the Courier Journal, died in the 1960's.

Mr. Dudley was a continuous resident of Flemingsburg from his birth to the time of his death, and he will be a fixture which no pressure can erase. A business man, he was among the most energetic and enterprising, and contributed largely to the improvement of the city in the matter of business houses and residences, a number of which he was the owner as the result of careful and economical business management and speculative foresight. He was also president of the Board of Trustees for the Flemingsburg Graded and High Schools for a number of years. Mr. Dudley had a grandson, Charles H. Dudley, who is a U. S. Marshal of the District Court of Lexington, Kentucky.

CHAPTER TWENTY-TWO

THE POWERS OF FLEMING COUNTY, KENTUCKY

John S. Power was born in Fleming County, Kentucky near the village of Mt. Gilead on the 13th day of June, 1842, and was the second child of five children — four sons and one daughter born to Richard and Mary Ann Hull Power. His father, Richard Power, was a native Kentuckian, born in 1813, of Revolutionary stock, whose immediate ancestors were Virginians and many who were participants in the American War of Independence against British oppression, and served conspicuously in many memorable engagements during the War.

Richard Power, father of John the subject of this sketch, moved from his home in Mt. Gilead when his son, John, was six years old, moving to the western part of the county and remaining there until John was fifteen years of age, where he attended the district common schools and acquired a fair knowledge of the rudiments of an English education. His father and family then moved to Mason County near the city of Maysville, where the son attended the Maysville Seminary conducted by Prof. William E. Richeson, a graduate of the University of Virginia. On leaving the Seminary, he enlisted in the Confederate States Army in the 2nd Ky. Battallion of Mounted Rifles, commanded by Lieut. Col. Thomas Johnson in which he served until the close of the War when he was surrendered with the command at Mt. Sterling, Kentucky, on the 2nd day of May, 1865. Upon his return home, he engaged in farming and teaching school, the latter with his brother, Joseph H. Power, near Lewisburg in Mason County, Ky. In the meantime, he entered upon the study of law and was admitted to the Bar at the April term in 1874 of the Mason Circuit Court.

On the 27th day of September, 1871, he was married to Miss Alice Bruce Dudley of Flemingsburg, Ky. who was the youngest of the children of Joseph and Harriet Bruce

93

Dudley, both of whom were descendants of Virginia families and natives of Fleming County. To this union was born seven children.

Mr. Power engaged in the practice of law alone until his brother, Joseph H. Power, was admitted to the Bar, then they entered into a partnership until the former was elected Judge of the Fleming County Court, then the partnership was dissolved. In 1876, he was appointed school Commissioner of Fleming County and served until 1878, when he resigned upon his election to the office of Judge of Fleming County Court, and to which he was re-elected in 1892. Upon the expiration of his term of office of County Judge, he resumed the practice of law in which he continued for many years.

The second part of this chapter will honor Joseph H. Power, the brother of John S. Power.

JOSEPH H. POWER
Attorney at Law, Flemingsburg, Kentucky

Joseph H. Power was born on the 23rd day of September, 1849 in the old Centerville Precinct in Fleming County, Kentucky. His father, Richard Power, was born and reared near Mt. Carmel, Fleming County, Kentucky; and his mother, Mary Hull, was born and reared in Mason County, Kentucky; his grandfather, John Power, was a native of Louden County, Virginia. When a small boy his father emigrated to Fleming County, Kentucky, where he reared a large family. Joseph Power, his great grandfather and six brothers joined the Continental Army and were at the surrender of Lord Cornwallis at Yorktown. Mr. Power, at the age of five years, removed with his father's family from Fleming County to near Maysville, Kentucky, where he lived with his parents on a farm and attended school for a few years at the old Maysville Seminary, conducted by Rand and Richeson, and where he received the principal part of his education. His family moved into the city of Maysville in the spring of 1860, where he resided until 1869. After leaving school, he engaged in teaching and was a clerk in a dry goods store in the city of Maysville until 1869, when he moved to a farm near Lewisburg in Mason County, Kentucky. He resided here until the spring of 1874, when he removed to Flemingsburg, Kentucky, and began the study of law in the office of his brother, Judge John S. Power. He procured license to practice law on the 18th day of February, 1876, and was admitted to the Fleming County Bar, but did not begin the practice until March, 1877, since which time he was actively engaged in the practice of his profession. He made a painstaking, successful lawyer and had a lucrative practice. He was elected to the office of County Attorney for Fleming County in August, 1886, and was re-elected in 1890, and held the position until January 1st, 1895.

On the 9th day of February, 1888, he was married to Miss Martha W. Robinson of Montgomery County, Kentucky, and to this union was born two sons, both who were reared in Flemingsburg, both educated in our local schools and also attended colleges of their choice. The elder son, Henry, was not known by the writer of this sketch, but I believe that he made his home in Chicago, Ill., or Racine, Wisconsin and his profession is not known to me. His younger son, Douglas, served with our armed forces in France with honor and when the war was over, he returned home with a beautiful French bride, and cared for his father in his remaining years. After his father's death, he and his wife disposed of all his property and moved to Chicago, Ill., where they are now living.

CHAPTER TWENTY-THREE

COUNTY AND CITY DIRECTORY
OF
FLEMING COUNTY, KENTUCKY IN
1871 - 1873

Circuit Court

Hon. R. H. Stanton _____ Circuit Judge

George T. Halbert _____ Commonwealth Attorney

H. B. Dobyns _____ Circuit Clerk

B. A. Plummer _____ Sheriff

    The Circuit Court convenes on the second Monday in February and August.

County Court

James E. Smith _____ County Judge

A. E. Cole _____ County Attorney

Mike M. Teager _____ County Clerk

B. A. Plummer _____ Sheriff

Alf. Norwood _____ Deputy Sheriff

Thomas H. Caywood _____ Deputy Sheriff

James Payne _____ Deputy Sheriff

John Morgan _____ Jailer

Mathew Thompson _____ Assessor

Charles Z. Duley _____ Coroner

Henry Lander _____ Surveyor

    The County Court meets the 4th Monday in every month.

    Quarterly Court meets the third Monday in March, June, September and December.

    The Court of Claims meets the 4th Monday in October.

Magistrates Courts

    1st District: Sherburne, John Roby and J. C. Mers, magistrates. James Vinkirk, constable. Courts held on the 4th Thursday and Saturday in March, June, September and December.

2nd District: Mt. Carmel, James Darnell and N. A. Glascock, magistrates. ———, constable. Courts held on the 1st and 3rd Saturdays in March, June, September and December.

3rd District: Mt. Carmel, James Darnell and N. A. magistrates. David S. Morrison, constable. Courts held on the 4th Tuesday and 4th Saturday in March, June, September and December.

4th District: Hillsboro, David R. Nealis and A. J. Royse, magistrates. Hiram Royse, constable. Courts held 3rd Saturday and 4th Friday in March, June, September and December.

5th District: Tilton, Elijah Thomas and James Cochran, magistrates. J. J. Thompson, constable. Courts held 4th Wednesday and 4th Friday in March, June, September and December.

6th District: Centerville, James H. Barton and W. W. Stockdale, magistrates. S. A. Caywood, constable. Courts held 3rd and 4th Saturdays in March, June, September and December.

7th District: Flemingsburg, L. F. Bright and M. W. Lyons, magistrates. E. L. Singleton, constable. Courts held 4th Friday and last Thursday in March, June, September and December.

8th District: Fox, J. H. Saunders and J. P. Luman, magistrates. C. H. Spradlin, constable. Courts held 3rd Thursday and 3rd Saturday in March, June, September and December.

9th District: Elizaville, William Garey and Isaac Plank, magistrates. John G. Adams, constable. Courts held 2nd Friday and 4th Saturday in March, June, September and December.

City Director

C. H. Ashton	Police Judge
H. O. Hammer	City Marshal
City Council	N. S. Andrews
James H. Dudley	M. W. Lyons
Wm. P. Fant	One vacancy

Town Church Directory

Presbyterian Church: Services every Sunday morning, Rev. J. P. Hendrick, pastor.

Prayer meeting every Wednesday night.

M. E. Church South: Services the 1st and 2nd Sundays in every month. Morning and evening. Rev. J. W. Wightman, pastor. Prayer meeting every Thursday night.

Christian Church: Services every Sabbath. Preaching every other Sabbath, Elder J. W. Cox, pastor. Prayer meeting Thursday night.

Catholic Church: Services 1st and 3rd Sundays in each month. Father John Hickey, pastor.

Episcopal Church: Services occasionally.

Baptist Church: Services every 2nd and 4th Sunday afternoons of each month at 3:30 p.m. Rev. Keys, pastor.

CHAPTER TWENTY-FOUR

BATH COUNTY KILLING

The Correct Statement of the Killing of Berry at Sharpsburg, 1872
(From The Mt. Sterling Sentinel)

"Our last issue contained an account of the killing of William Berry, at Sharpsburg, Ky., on the 16th inst. which to some extent, as we have since learned to be incorrect.

On the 15th inst. Berry, while intoxicated, shot at Adam Trumbo twice without effect. For this he was arrested by the Deputy Sheriff and placed in charge of Richard Withers and Cole Bascom as guards and remained in charge on the following night.

On the morning of the 16th, he was brought to Sharpsburg by Cole Bascom for trial, being still under guard and disarmed; and while he was hitching his horse a few yards distant, Adam Trumbo, the father-in-law and Jake Trumbo, the brother-in-law of Berry, attacked him while hitching his horse with his face from them. The one with a shotgun loaded with balls, the other with a pistol, and before his guard could reach the spot, put eleven bullets in him.

The Deputy Sheriff, Mr. Elgin, apprehending danger to Berry, had sometime before the killing told Adam Trumbo that Berry was in his custody, disarmed and that he must not trouble him. Trumbo assured Sheriff Elgin that he would not interfere with Berry and went as straight as he could to the house where his son was waiting, and both proceeded to where the tragedy occurred, and shot the prisoner down, as above stated, without a word of warning or giving him an opportunity to defend himself.

The deceased was a young man and belonging to one of the most wealthy and respectable families in the county. About January, 1870, he by deed of gift conveyed to his wife, the daughter of Adam Trumbo, $30,000 worth of land, being about all he was worth after payment of his debts and since

99

then, as we learned, they have lived unhappily, she having left him before the killing.

We give no opinion as to the innocence or guilt of the Trumbos as they have been arrested and were to be tried at Sharpsburg yesterday, but the relation of the parties render it a horrid case.

Messrs. J. M. Nesbit, County Attorney of Bath County, William L. Holt, Richard Reid and J. S. Hurt will appear as attorneys in the prosecution, and Messrs. Reid and Stone, V. B. Young and B. D. Luvy in the defence."

CHAPTER TWENTY-FIVE

CHARLES H. LAWSON, RETAIL DRUGGIST
OF FLEMINGSBURG, KENTUCKY

The drug establishment of Charles H. Lawson, located on Water Street in the Ryan Building (now houses the grocery store of Bob Klee and residence of Mrs. Marshall Berry, each owning their own property), was one of the most eligible business localities in the city, yet under the business of the young proprietor, it soon took a stand as a business point of view in successful competition with the older houses of its kind.

Mr. Lawson was born April 23rd, 1870 in Fleming County, Kentucky, raised on a farm until 1885 or 1886, when he at a very young age engaged in the livery business with his brother, J. W. Lawson, in Flemingsburg. He was a young man of excellent habits, quiet, steady and a thoughtful business man, immersed in the matters of his own affairs, gentlemanly, courteous and attentive to a degree that he could not fail to succeed. After the experience in the drug business for three years, his thought was that he might thoroughly qualify himself in his chosen line, he entered the Louisville School of Pharmacy, September 16th, 1895. In 1896, he passed the required state examination successfully and was duly registered as a practicing pharmacist. Thus equipped in the special line of his profession, he was prepared to give special attention to all prescriptions intrusted to his care and preparation.

In June, 1899, he purchased the drug business of Dr. H. C. Kehoe to which he added a complete line of drugs, stationery and toilet articles. By force of industry and enterprise together with a close attention to business in all its details in an almost incredibly short space of time, he built up a trade that deserved an honorable and successful business accomplished by a judicious investment of capital and a strict adherence to good and steady business habits.

CHAPTER TWENTY-SIX

FIGHTING
THE 16TH VOL. INFANTRY U.S.A.

Fight The War Over, But No Blood Shed

(An interesting clipping which is not dated, but probably between 1870 and 1880)

The fourth annual re-union of the 16th Kentucky Volunteer Infantry and survivors of the Battle of Franklin, Tenn. ocurred in Flemingsburg, last Thursday under the direction of Jos. Dudley Post No. 71 G. A. R. The 16th saw service which culminated in the Battle of Franklin, Tenn., which event they annually celebrate.

The day opened up bright and clear and the early morning train brought in about twenty-five of the "Boys" and a delegation of the Women's Relief Corps, while others came through by "land"; though not in "web-foot style" but sure enough riding things.

At 10:00 o'clock the Association was called to order by Capt. M. C. Hutchins of Maysville, president, and Comrade Jos. I. Dorsey of Flemingsburg was called to the Secretary's chair. The following veterans of time as well as of "war" answered the roll call. They were:

Company A

Elias Young, Ewing	J. T. Robb, Sardis
Geo. Berz, Mayslick	P. Walton, Washington
C. Paul, Maysville	J. Burns, Oakwoods

Company B

W. A. Gooding, Wall'ford	Geo. Ross, Wallingford
J. Hammond, Sandford	W. K. Ham, Sandford
E. W. Bell, Johnson	G. McDonald, Carlisle
S. P. Gully, Wallingford	E. H. Jones, Sandford
W. Fern, Wallingford	Jas. Hurst Wallingford

J. E. Hurst, Sandford

Company C

T. A. Tearum, Okl   W. Chisholm, Mayslick
W. B. Dawson, Mayslick

Company D

O. Bongham, Johns'lle   C. Little, Lonoxburg

Company E

G. Clinger, Maysville   Wm. Cox, Augusta
B. Weaver, Augusta   A. Martin, Millersburg

Company G

W. Steele, Wedonia

Company H

T. Y. Wood, Tilton   J. L. Overley, Tilton
R. S. Finley, Tilton   W. B. Scott, Bethel
J. Cogar, Mayslick   T. W. Coaper, Nepton
L. W. Hess, Illinois   W. F. Hendrick, Flem'burg
J. I. Dorsey, Flemin'burg J. P. Dorsey, Flemin'burg
J. P. Hendrick, Flem'burg C. L. Overley, Maysville
J. L. Dorsey, Elizaville   H. W. Hall, Carlisle

The following officers were elected for the ensuing year: President, C. L. Overley, Maysville; Historian, L. W. Hess, Elkart, Illinois; Secretary, G. M. Clinger, Maysville; Treasurer, T. J. Wood, Tilton; Chaplain, Rev. J. P. Hendrick, Flemingsburg. Augusta was selected as the next "objective point." Promptly at noon Comrade R. S. Hudson appeared on the stage bearing the banner of the Jos. Dudley Post and on their behalf invited first the 16th Kentucky U.S.A. survivors, and then all the old soldiers of both sides of all wars with their wives and children to a "Bean Bake" at the Post's quarters. The line was formed and old soldiers fell in to the number of 162 followed by their families. The "Bean Bake" consisted of turkey, ham, hot coffee, oysters, fried and escalloped, salads, pies, cakes, etc.

Daughters of the grim and grizzled old "Vets" waiting on the tables added grace and beauty to the occasion. After the dinner was over our own John P. McCartney delivered

103

an address of welcome, which was eloquently responded to by Capt. M. C. Hutchins of Maysville. Chaplain Hendrick then introduced Elder Wm. Stanley who was a gallant aide on the staff of General Jno. B. Hood C.A.S., and the way his remarks were received, showed that indeed the War was over with those present with much handshaking and many tender memories of those who had answered the last "Tattoo," the re-union dissolved, each voting this one a success and promising to meet at Augusta next year unless*

> The muffled drum's sad roll has beat
> The soldier's last tattoo,
> No more on life's parade shall meet that
> Brave and gallant few.
> On fame's eternal camping ground their
> Silent tents are spread,
> And glory guards with solemn 'round
> The bivouac of the dead.

*Written in fine print at the bottom of this article.

CHAPTER TWENTY-SEVEN

A LETTER FROM J. T. WALKER OF GREENSBORO, GEORGIA APRIL 8, 1882

Mr. Editor: Seeing in the Democrat of the 6th inst. mention of the interment of Mrs. Blanton at the old Brick Union Cemetery, brings up memories of the long, long ago. More than half a century ago, the writer of this letter witnessed the interment of Mrs. David Howe, who had died from injuries received by a fall from a horse, and her son or nephew, who was the son-in-law of Jno. Armstrong, and perhaps others not now remembered. This occurred in 1827 when I was seven years old and attending school at the old church, taught by Delano R. (now Judge) Eckles of Indiana. Of the pupils there were Bob Anderson, John Secrest, John VanSant, Jno. Warrick, Sam Weaver, and his sisters, Amanda, Sophia and Cynthia, Sallie Leaper, Harriet Smith, Capt. Tuggles' children, Mcilvaine's children, William Armstrong's children, and others I cannot recall. The ministers I used to hear in the old Church besides our teacher, were Northcutt and Osburn and Henry Robertson, who would sometimes exhort. After an absence of fifty years, I revisited the old site and found the church in ruins — the supposed work of an incendiary. Of this old school, John VanSant, Dr. Armstrong, Thos. Sutton, Billy Hendrick and Mrs. R. Thomas (nee Smith) were all that I met who were fellow pupils in Joseph Adair's school taught in the same neighborhood the year before where I learned my ABC's. My home at that time was with my grandfather, Aurelius Walker, who lived where Robert Armstrong lived and died. As the place of my birth and the home of my childhood my affections are closely united and, while memory lasts, I will cherish the fondest recollection of the place and people, having reached my three score years, I am the last one of the name, born on Kentucky soil. Since my visit in 1870, many of my dear relatives of this place have been called away, viz., my uncle John N. Proctor, Elijah Thomas, Mrs. Sallie and Margaret Collier, Mrs. Walker, Jno. H. Wells, his noble wife and son, William, Dr. Cook and his daughter, Mrs. Hord. Of my friends were Messrs. F. Robertson, Moses Hord, Billy Hendrick, Isaiah Dent, Robert Armstrong, George Summers and others not remembered who have paid the debt — Peace to their ashes.

(So wrote J. T. Walker of Greensboro, Georgia in 1882).

CHAPTER TWENTY-EIGHT

MARRIAGES FOR THE YEAR OF 1883

The following is a list of the marriages solemnized in Fleming County, Ky., during the year of 1883, together with the date of occurrence. Also deaths in 1883.

Day   January
1—James A. Kincaid, Mollie Kincaid
3—Chas. D. Kissick, Anozetta Fox
4—John W. Bateman, Malinda Breeze
4—Wm. M. Ingrham, Eliaebath McKee
5—Fleming R. Johnson, Jennie Hiner
6—Wm. W. Cook, Mary J. Summers
14—Wm. H. Humphries, Martha Hartley
16—Patrick B. Todd, Annie B. Evans
17—Wm. E. Clarke, Catherine McSweeny
18—Albert Crain, Cora B. Harman
18—Sam C. Grose, Rebecca Saunders
22—Ira T. Goodwin, Sarah A. Saunders
23—I. M. Swim, Amanda Price
25—A. C. Saunders, Emily Hopkins

Day   February
8—Geo. Yazel, Amelia Heflin
20—Linsey Jordan, Ecybindy Saunders
22—Allen Kieth, Nannie W. Todd
Day   March
3—R. P. Million, Florence V. Martin
9—John Mitchell, Susan Richards
13—John G. James, Betsy Luman
18—Francis M. Stockdale, Cecila Stockdale
22—Sousley Harmon, Lois J. Emmons
29—Jerome W. Breeze, Martha A. Vinson
29—Wm. Quaintance, Mary K. Dudley
29—Jas. B. Ashbrook, Mary J. Coulthard

Day   April
2—R. M. Cralie, Mary Wall
5—Wm. C. Washburn, Virginia Peck
11—Jas. D. Pierce, Margarte Emmons
12—N. B. Erskin, Louisa V. Rolph
19—John B. Thompson, Mary V. Tevgybough
20—R. K. Ewan, Barbara C. Herritt
24—Robt. Helphestine, Emily R. Faris
27—Major E. Jordon, Cathernie Gorman

Day   May
10—John A. Allen, Nannie Hendrickson
13—Dan'l B. Reeves, Eliza J. Rogers
15—Wm. A. Wiggins, Virginia A. Swain
17—Geo. W. McIntosh, Eliza Hughes
17—W. F. Rolph, Harriet E. Ham
24—John Linville, Catherine Arnold
24—Chas. W. Rice, Mary F. Heath

Day   June
4—Sam'l P. Walton, Miranda Barton
12—John W. Foxworthy, Mary E. Wallingford
20—Wm. D. Estill, Enola A. Beckett
20—John S. McElroy, Nannie Vanzant
25—J. R. Crain, Lou Nettie Scrudder

Day   July
4—Alex. Bowling, Rosanna Page
12—John Speakman, Sarah E. Perry
19—John W. Coyle, Lura D. Wheeler
25—Sam'l Richey, Mary E. Mulligan
26—M. F. Triplett, Lydia E. Mallory
Day   August
22—Wm. C. Payne, V. Amelia Crain
27—Burgess D. Humphries, Rebecca Martin

Day   September
4—Alex. Truesdale, Georetta Hedges

6—Franklin Vinson, Annie Carpenter
17—Daniel B. Hinton, Sarah B. Story
17—Thos. H. Walton, Annie E. Williamson
18—Isaac M. Evans, Mina L. Campbell
18—Jas. D. Peck, Bettie J. Shepard
20—Basil Harman, Jenni Todd
22—Silas O. Duncan, Nettie M. Mills
24—J. M. Turner, Nancy E. Wallingford
24—A. A. Kenner, Letha B. Adams
24—Oscar B. Warrick, Annie B. Calvert
25—Wm. Busby, Alice Smoot
26—Simpson T. Holland, Jennie K. Shultz

Day   October
 3—W. B. Trumbo, Bettie B. Armstrong
 6—Chas. R. Garr, Sallie R. Grain
10—Wm. T. Standfield, Delila J. Bartlett
15—W. T. Eubanks, Cleo J. Benton
16—J. H. Darnall, Mary Strother
22—James Planck, Alice D. Sims
22—Jermiah Ham, Elizebath Mead
22—Ambrose D. Harmon, Ida Daily
26—Walyer B. Dearing, Ida Chapman
27—Thomas Vice, Maraget M. Faris
30—Jerimah Carpenter, Lucianda Hinton
30—Harrison M. Baugh, Elizabeth R. Breeze
30—Jas. R. Breeze, Mattie F. Baugh
31—Bruce B. Stone, Eliza D. Adkinson

Day   November
 6—Aylett R. Amos, Elizabeth T. Hendrick
20—Sam'l M. Luman, Mary Taylor
21—John W. Zorn, Sarah T. Hughes
28—John A. Powell, Adaline Adams
29—John F. Mitchell, Sarah E. Watkins
29—Francis B. Thomas, Lourana Gibbs

Day   December
 5—Wm. Stanfield, Nancy J. Ervin

10—J. C. Crawford, Sarah K. McRoberts
11—B. O. McGregor, Martha Jones
12—John P. Darnall, Mary Andrews
12—Dunlap Howe, Lizzie Lee Stitt
18—A. A. Hood, Emily A. Belt
19—John Hughes, Zadie A. McCord
20—Eli Williams, Barbara E. Overley
23—Chas. P. Vice, Autha Littleton
25—John Sapp, Elizabeth Thomas
25—John Stasey, Mary H. Dyer
27—Jasper N. Reeves, Minnie Wightman
27—Fantley R. Hopkins, Nancy J. Planck
27—Hardiman B. Williams, Mary J. Rankin
27—Ezra Elrod, Ella Conard
27—Chas. W. Peters, Rosa H. Alexander

BURIALS IN FLEMING COUNTY CEMETERY 1893

Date of Interment, Name, Residence, Disease

January 1st, Wm. Regan, Flemingsburg, heart disease.
January 3rd, Mrs. H. G. Evans, County, gen'l debility.
March 5th, Mrs. Zimmerman, County, dropsy.
March 18th, Wm. R. McIlvain, County, pneumonia.
March 22nd, Seth Botts, Flemingsburg, consumption.
March 30th, Mrs. Mary W. Crain, County, consumption.
April 4th, Ernest Lee, County, congestion.
April 8th, Daugherty (infant), Sherburne, croup.
April 15th, Thos. M. Allen, Augusta, Ky., accident.
April 25th, Lillie Lightfoot, Flemingsburg, scarlet fever.
April 25th, J. B. Zimmerman, County, old age.
April 26th, T. C. Tirner, Huntington, W. Va., congestion
April 26th, Mrs. H. B. Dudley, Flemingsburg, old age.
May 4th, R. T. McDonald, Flemingsburg, consumption.
May 9th, John S. Lightfoot, Flemingsburg, scarlet fever.
May 12th, Mrs. E. J. Logan, Poplar Plains, pneumonia.
June 15th, Lucy A. Knight, Elizaville, consumption.
June 15th, Geo. P. Dulin, County, heart disease.
June 28th, Jerry Hall, County, old age.

110

June 29th, C. A. Ashton, Flemingsburg, scarlet fever.

June 30th, Geo. F. Dudley, Flemingsburg, scarlet fever.

June 30th, Lizzy M. Dudley, Flemingsburg, scarlet fever.

June 30th, Mrs. M. Washburn, County, pneumonia.

August 4th, Dr. W. W. McDowell, Flemingsburg, consumption.

August 23rd, Emma Harrison, Flemingsburg, scarlet fever.

August 25th, Mrs. M. Dickson, Maysville, Ky., cancer

August 26, —— Tillett, Flemingsburg, ————.

September 21st, Geo. W. Denny, Flemingsburg, ————.

September 27th, John H. Vanzant, Elizaville, malarial fever.

October 2nd, Selman Williams, County, consumption.

October 30th, Mrs. T. A. Couser, County, ————.

November 1st, W. S. Botts, Flemingsburg, general debility.

November 10th, Mrs. B. A. Cavan, Flemingsburg, general debility.

November 18th, Ina Myers, P. L. Mills, Croup.

November 25th, Joseph Troop, Poplar Plains, heart disease.

November 27, Jennie McCartney, Flemingsburg, ————.

December 11th, Ed O'Sullivan, Flemingsburg, Consumption.

Colored List

March 15th, Mrs. M. Sermons, Flemingsburg, Consumption.

May 2nd, Geo. N. Harrison, Flemingsburg, pneumonia.

May 18th, Mrs. Patsey Coleman, Flemingsburg ————.

May 31st, Mrs. Brown, Flemingsburg,————.

July 1st, Ben Lyon, County, pneumonia.

July 20th, Asa Farrow, County, Consumption.

August 23rd, Mrs. A. Jenkins, Flemingsburg, Malaria.

September 10th, Geo. W. Jenkins, Flemingsburg, malaria.

September 11th, John W. Smith, County, worms.

October 4th, Vina D. Crump, Flemingsburg, ————.

October 26th, Nannie Bush, Flemingsburg, ————
November 13th, Ika Herndon, Flemingsburg, pneumonia
Removals from other Cemeteries to Flemingsburg
Ada McIlvain from Andrews
Samuel Darnall from Darnall's
Thos. J. Hall from Brick Union
C. Pumphrey from Lake Stockton
David Howe from Brick Union
Geo. Barnes from Lake Stockton
J. C. Washburn from U. B. Licks
Mr. M. Darnall from Darnall's
Martha Darnall from Darnall's
Mrs. M. Hall from Brick Union
Willie Pumphrey from Lake Stockton
Joseph Dudley from Lake Stockton
———— McDowell from Presbyterian
Mrs. E. Barnes from Lake Stockton
Minnie G. Kenner from Maysville

> The Honorable
> George Faulkner, Superintendent

CHAPTER TWENTY-NINE

MARRIAGES FOR THE YEAR OF 1895

Day   January
1—M. Conrad, Annie Arnold
1—M. S. Littlejohn, Nannie E. Payne
8—Lee Lewis, Viola Crawford
8—S. M. Hurst, Minnie Marshall
9—J. J. Baxter, Ruthie McKee
9—A. N. Selby, Dora B. Arnold
17—B. F. Ishmael, Dora Harmon
22—T. B. Vice, Lizzie B. Trumbo
22—W. H. Graham, Lide Williams
23—Thos. McKee, Georgia Arnold
23—Chas. G. Planck, Jennie A. Fitch
24—Elias W. May, Marteela Boyd
29—J. M. Brown, Inza Prater
29—Odd Hunt, Laura Bohannon

Day   February
5—Wm. Bradford, Rebecca Jackson
12—Isaac Blanton, Mary Murphy
12—Wm. F. Watson, Annie E. Porter
13—A. T. Alexander, Sarah R. Bell
18—J. F. Lukins, Eliza Umstattd
18—C. P. Williams, Mary T. Baird
19—J. E. Alexander, Adah Caywood
21—J. W. Shockley, Amanda Faris
21—J. R. Rose, Jannie Rankins
25—J. W. Hysong, Sarah Turner
26—L. F. Humphries, Hettie Martin.
27—L. C. Brown, Cynthia Poynter

Day   March
4—J. T. Smart, Dora B. Rice
6—H. Helphinstine, Polly A. Reeves

18—C. F. Parker, Matilda Hildreth
20—W. H. Standiford, Mary E. Sapp
21—Benj Estep, A. Gardner
22—J. F. Gardner, Dora Gulley
25—Daniel Hall, Annie M. McVey
26—T. J. Wiggins, Bertie Bramel
27—Steph'n Hatfiels, Hattie Payne

Day   April
 2—C. G. Lytle, Mattie Cotterill
 2—Paul Foalmar, N. Armstrong
 6—Grant Posten, Mary Mitchell
 8—Sam'l Earles, H. J. Thompson
 8—G. W. Gardner, Mary Earles
10—John Estep, Ida Henderson
16—J. M. Hunter, Mattie T. Jones

Day   May
 7—J. W. Lawson, Lula E. Crain
 8—Jas. Mairel, Mag Lawrence
11—E. K. Cameron, Dallas Eaton
16—J. F. Lewman, Sarah Royse
17—Frank E. Boys, Fannie Harmon
22—L. E. Swetnam, Fannie Jackson
25—Lewis Newdigate, Mary E. McKee
27—J. D. Florence, R. J. Grayson
27—G. A. Muse, Cordia Brammer
27—C. F. DeBell, Bertie Hudson
29—J. M. Doyle, Hattie Hurst
30—H. Smart, Nettie Atchison

Day   June
18—M. D. Ray, Bettie M. Stoutt
18—Jas. Cummings, Emma Moore
25—Eli Williams, Mattie ————

Day   July
 3—Jno. K. Poynter, Nancy Steele
30—W. B. Washburn, Mar A. Timmons

114

Day   August
1—W. H. Bentley, Lida F. Vice
5—Geo. Faulkner, Isabel Newcome
22—W. B. Dugan, Nancy Whisman
26—Thos. Saunders, Jane D. Nealis
26—Columb' Callahan, Eva Sipple
26—Rob't J. Hinton, Arthusia Cochran

Day   September
2—W. J. Alexander, Julia T. Caywood
2—Claude Reeves, Nettie Jordan
2—Jos. Conners, Delia Kinney
4—R. L. Porter, E. A. Moren
5—J. B. Glascock, Alice Foxworthy
5—J. H. Nixon, Am'd Crawford
11—D. P. Dye, Amie B. Wise
11—L. C. Demaree, Fannie Lander
12—Norman Massie, Emma Griffy
13—Alfred Lynam, Cin'd Kenney
21—J. W. West, Lizzie L. Clark
25—Carl Speasmaker, Mar Burns
25—W. O. Tribby, Laura Crawford
25—L. Crawford, Lucinda Lykins
26—Andrew Smalley, Perlina Niece
30—R. Carpenter, Lizzie Hopkins

Day   October
2—E. E. Hopkins, Amanda Gray
2—T. J. Smoot, Emma Gardner
2—Jas. Reynolds, Mary Brown'
7—Jno. Skaggs, Cyn Foudray
8—T. S. King, Bessie Carpenter
14—Jno. S. Peck, Lizzie Dorsey
15—Millard Cooper, Jennie Daulton
21—S. A. Faris, Myrtle Kendall
24—Benj Smart, Isabella Jolly
29—Geo. A. Pepper, Osa Biddle
30—Chas. Denton, Mary Traylor
30—V. F. McCord, Bertie Bishop

Day   *November*
4—Leander Jones, Carrie L. Clive
4—Mont Arnold, Lula Waltz
5—Thos. H. Dudley, Lida Scruggs
5—W. D. Call, Lina Phelps
9—Jno. S. Hinton, Rosa Hartman
12—Jonas Crump, Martha Cooper
13—W. M. McCarty, Mollie McClure
14—Geo Jones, Sarah Pettit
15—B. B. Markwell, Myrtle Elrod
19—C. W. Newdigate, A. F. McKee
20—S. C. Kelley, Nolla Sutton
20—Chas J. Sutton, Lettie Barksdale
21—Wallace Sapp, Lillie Corey
27—J. C. Hughbanks, Rebecca McCord
29—Jno Williams, Addah Hawes
29—M. J. Breen, Katie A. Ryan

Day   *December*
2—W. H. Muse, Mary Brammer
10—John Flora, E. Alexander
10—W. W. Hedger, F. F. Lemmons
11—Sam'l Hall, Sallie Jordan
11—Lewis Ishmael, May Johnson
16—S. J. Daugherty, Anna Waugh
16—Gano Hendrix, Arthusia Blair
18—Geo Boyd, Corcie Johnson
18—I. F. Fizer, Louisa Kirk
18—S. F. Hinton, Mary Barnes
18—H. C. Galbraith, Edna C. West
19—B. N. Houston, Eliza Davenport
23—Jno H. Rigdon, Nannie Colville
23—Chas F. Berry, Laura LeForge
23—H. F. Lewman, Sarah A. Petty
23—J. T. Alexander, Lola Evans

BURIALS IN THE FLEMING COUNTY CEMETERY 1895
January 9th, W. S. E. Belt, County
January 18th, Samuel Anderson, City

January 26th, Anna D. VanSant, Johnson
January 28th, Amos Kelley, Johnson
February 1st, Joshua Dudley, Maysville
February 3rd, Overley (infant), Athens
February 9th, John Heron, County
February 23rd, Mrs. Nancy Early, County
February 25th, Mrs. Jennie Saunders, Paris
February 27th, Mrs. Jennie Washburne, County
March 12th, Nathan H. Jones, City
March 13th, Henry Kissick, County
March 26th, Mrs. Margaret H. McConnell, Louisville
April 4th, Wm. H. Whaley, County
April 7th, Frank W. Allen, Augusta
April 10th, Warren Ringo McIntyre, County
May 30th, T. P. Dorsey (infant son), County
June 12th, J. Bennett McIntyre, Newport
June 13th, Mrs. Juliet Sudduth, City
June 21st, Mrs. Jane Armstrong, City
June 26th, Chas. W. Shockley, Crains
July 16th, E. L. Fant, City
August 7th, John Dawson, County
August 8th, Dan H. Paxton (infant), County
August 28th, Mrs. Caroline W. Newcombe, Bath County
September 9th, Marion G. Hinton, Plummers Landing
September 23rd, Mrs. Martha A. Sims, City
October 9th, Mrs. Valeria Grannis, City
October 15th, Maud Royse, Sandford
November 2nd, Mrs. Rebecca H. Amos, City
November 4th, Mrs. Lizzie VanSant, City
November 5th, W. H. Fischer (infant), City
November 7th, Sallie Cullen, County
November 7th, Harrison Warren, City
November 12th, Edna Bruce Ewan, Helena
November 24th, R. R. Luman (infant), Ashland
December 4th, Joshua B. Glascock, City
December 15th, Mrs. Fannie H. McCreary, City
December 23, Mrs. Lydia M. Hall, Wedonia
December 31, Martin Breen (infant), City

CHAPTER THIRTY

THE LIFE OF JAMES P. HENDRICK, THE PRESBYTERIAN

This work was sold to raise funds for a fitting monument to the memory of James P. Hendrick and was handled by W. H. Barksdale, Flemingsburg, Kentucky; Dr. A. M. Wallingford, Mt. Carmel; Dr. John T. VanSant, Paris; Dr. James A. VanSant, Mt. Sterling; and W. H. Means, Maysville.

In regard to this book The Presbyterian of Philadelphia of May 1st says: "This, a volume of 342 pages (octavo) giving an interesting history of civil affairs and of Presbyterianism in Kentucky from 1850 to 1898. The reader is at once charmed with the character and life of the subject and the manner in which the author has done his work. Dr. Hendrick was one of a noble generation, who sat at the feet of such men as the Breckinridges, The Humpreys, John C. Young, Erastus McMasters and many others with a gifted intellect and such training. No wonder that he figured prominently in the arena when the declaration and testimony required in the church of God, men of piety, principle and decision. Having espoused as a matter of duty the cause of the Union in the Civil War, although himself a slave-holder and a Democrat, he was known not only as a devoted minister and chaplain, but also as the fighting Parson.

"The volume traces his early life, his days in Centre College, Danville, Kentucky of which he was afterwards for twenty-five years one of its trustees and chief supporters. His call to work in Texas where he spent a year, and his settlement in Carlisle and Flemingsburg, Kentucky where, both as a teacher and a preacher, he was a 'Prince in Israel,' until his lamented death.

"The author has given some specimens of his sermons and some extracts from a volume of 'Forms of Prayer,' suited for family worship in which the scholar and the man of prayer are always prominent, as well as some charming

118

letters from Europe, written while abroad as a delegate to the Pan-Presbytrian Council at Belfast, Ireland.

"As a model life for young ministers, as well as a valuable contribution to history, the author has done good service not only to his family and friends, but to the church of which he was so honored a servant. The volume reads like a romance and one beginning its perusal will be likely to finish it before laying it aside."

The Herald and Presbyter of April 17th says: "This is an admirably prepared biography of a great and good man. Dr. Hendrick was a Presbyterian minister of Kentucky who labored in the ministry of the gospel for many years, and who was called away in 1898 after having attained the ripe old age of three score years and ten. This volume is a beautiful and dignified tribute to his memory, containing an outline of his life and labors, several sermons, addresses and letters, an account of the funeral services, his History of Ebenezer Presbytery, and many other matters interesting and appropriate. It is a volume that will be highly prized by the many loving and devoted relatives and friends of this noble man of God."

In 1898 Dr. Hendrick at his home on Kalamont baptized Ben Harbeson, the small son of Judge James P. Harbeson, who proved to be the last person that he ever baptized, for he died soon after.

The house that Dr. Hendrick lived in on Kalamont in Flemingsburg and which he remodeled to suit the need for living and teaching, is now (1967) the stately home of Mr. Kelley Vice and his family. Mr. Vice is employed at the Farmers Deposit Bank in Flemingsburg. Also at this date (September 27, 1967) the home that Dr. Hendrick lived in on West Water Street is now owned by Miss Marjorie Harmon, who is a teacher in our High School at Flemingsburg, and is occupied by her and her mother, Mrs. R. G. Harmon. The farm which Dr. Hendrick owned near the city limits and what was once Stockton Station, now belongs to Mr. Robert W. Crain, who with his land holdings, Tobacco Warehouseman and co-owner of the Flemingsburg Stockyards, is one of

Fleming County's most prominent business men.

Dr. Hendrick's Students of the Period of 1855-1887

In alphabetical order, I will name some of Dr. Hendrick's pupils who have been prominent men and women of Fleming County. The list contains between 450 and 500. If anyone desires to check on other pupils of Dr. Hendrick, the writer can furnish the entire list as the record states.

Harry Andrews
Alice Andrews
Phoebe Andrews
Thos. S. Andrews
Watson Andrews
Robert Andrews
Rose Alexander
Iolene Ashton
Jack Babbitt
Robert Babbitt
W. H. Barksdale
Dennis Belt
Amy Botts
Seth Botts
Thos. Botts
Chas. Burns
Enoch Burns
Eliza Cooper
Jas. Crane
Thos. Cushman
C. H. Darnell
Jas. C. Darnell
Amy Darnell
Wm. G. Dearing
Stockwell Dudley
Wm. Dorsey
Abner H. Evans
Lula Fant
Mattie Faulkner
Dan Fischer

Wm. Fischer
Thos. M. Fleming
John Fleming
Chas. Fleming
Julia Fleming
Add D. Fleming
Wat Fleming
John Fitch
Andrew Fountain
Wm. Fountain
Harry Foxworthy
H. B. Franklin
Squire Glasscock
Joseph Glasscock
Bruce Grannis
Jas. K. Grannis
Jack Grannis
Jerry Hall
Wm. P. Harbeson
Jas. P. Harbeson, Jr.
Joseph Hendrick
J. Paul Hendrick
Lizzie Hendrick
Wm. J. Hendrick
T. Hord
Lee Howe
Fannie Howe
Robt. Hudson
Mary Harbeson
Huston Hart

Penolope Hendrick
Horace January
N. O. Kendall
Rose Lander
Lutie Lee
Jesse Lee
Thos. Lee
Pearce Lightfoot
M. Markwell
John P. McCartney
Andrew McCartney
Jas. H. McCartney
Chas. D. McCartney
John McIlvane
John McHugh
Anna McMullin
Chas. Nute
Mahala Overton
Edward Pearce
Nellie Purvis
Frank Peed
Chas. Robertson
Wm. Robb
George Rogers
Eliza Ringo

Jas. Ryan
Wm. Rogers
Henry Rhodes
Mary Ryan
A. Sharp
Wm. M. Staggs
Jas. Spencer
J. P. Singleton
Sallie Smith
James Smith
Jane Stockwell
B. B. Stone
Maggie Sudduth
Bessie Sudduth
Belle Summers
L. Saddler
Sallie Shanklin
Wm. Smith
Chas. Summers
John Summers
John T. Vansant
Amanda Wall
Jas. Yantis
Maggie Yantis
These and many others

CHAPTER THIRTY-ONE

BALDWIN PIANO OFFICIAL

Dwight H. Baldwin died at the age of 78 years at his home in Cincinnati, O. He was of the firm of D. H. Baldwin & Co., one of Cincinnati's most widely known and largest manufacturers and dealers in pianos and organs in the west. At one time he was an itinerant music teacher, and in 1844 he married Miss Emerine Summers at Elizaville in Fleming County. She was a sister of Prof. Jesse Summers. It is said that he once broke rock on the pike via Paris and Maysville.

In a newspaper account in 1899 the will of D. H. Baldwin was contested by his widow. He left her an income of $5,000 a year for life and left most of his fortune to Presbyterian Missions. His estate was said to be worth $250,000. As they had no children, some Fleming County people would stand a good chance to inherit from her.

In the will of Mrs. D. H. Baldwin, nee Summers, who died in Cincinnati, it was reported she left $75,000 to Miss Jessie Summers, formerly of Elizaville, but this was reported as a rumor and without guarantee of its truth.

CHAPTER THIRTY-TWO

THE VOTE OF FLEMING CO., KY. NOVEMBER 6, 1894

Precincts	Congress		A.J.	Co. Judge		Clerk	Att'y.	Sheriff		Assessor		Jailer		Suv'r.	Cor'r.
	HART, Dem.	PUGH, Rep.	PAYNTER, Dem.	BOOE, Dem.	HUDSON, Rep.	McCREARY, Dém.	DEARING, Dem.	FOUNTAIN, Dem.	COLLIVER, Rep.	SMITH, Dem.	STAGGS, Rep.	SAUNDERS, Dem.	COLLINS, Rep.	COULTER, Dem.	GRIMES, Dem.
Sherburne	86	104	81	81	101	82	82	73	110	83	102	76	109	80	80
Tilton	159	89	147	146	93	155	152	146	92	153	87	150	90	145	145
Battle Run	92	74	94	99	68	98	97	96	70	97	69	94	72	93	94
Elizaville	150	78	161	159	78	161	159	160	76	162	76	157	80	157	159
Plummer's	57	114	62	62	112	62	62	62	112	62	111	60	114	62	62
Muses	39	181	34	37	176	35	34	63	158	35	176	35	178	33	33
Hillsboro	127	122	123	125	122	125	124	117	132	127	121	128	120	122	122
Grange City	74	140	76	76	140	76	74	76	141	76	140	76	140	75	76
Popular Plains	149	126	133	139	121	138	138	130	133	132	130	140	123	130	131
Wallingford	15	137	15	15	135	14	15	17	133	14	136	15	135	14	14
Court House	183	202	180	185	191	187	186	190	189	185	187	160	216	181	180
Clerk's Office	196	129	192	193	119	196	192	190	124	194	122	176	138	191	191
Fairview	148	65	151	152	60	152	150	151	61	150	62	150	63	149	151
Ewing	140	77	140	141	77	140	141	138	82	140	77	141	77	137	139
Mt. Carmel															
No. 15															
No. 16															
Mt. Carmel	173	191	181	182	186	182	177	185	183	182	186	175	199	179	175
Johnson	37	37	38	40	36	38	39	40	35	40	34	38	37	38	39
Totals	1825	1866	1808	1832	1815	1844	1833	1834	1831	1832	1816	1772	1891	1772	1791
Majorities		41		17				3		16			119		

CHAPTER THIRTY-THREE

DR. JOHN J. REYNOLDS, DRUGGIST.

THE ODDFELLOWS BUILDING OF FLEMINGSBURG, KENTUCKY — THE OLD AND NEW BUILDING

Oddfellows Will Remodel Their Old Building

On a Tuesday night in February, 1902, the members of Fleming Lodge No. 30, 1.O.O.F. of this city decided to tear down their building on the corner of Main Cross and Water Streets, and on the site erect a handsome three story brick building. The new building occupies a floor space of 39 x 89 feet, extending from the corner to the Dudley Block and was a modern structure at that time. The plans were drawn some time before by an experienced architect. On the ground floor there are three large store rooms and a seven foot stairway. Under one of the rooms is a large basement laid in concrete and well lighted. The second floor is divided into ten office rooms and a seven foot hallway, all beautifully decorated. The third floor was then, and has continued to be, used as the Main Lodge Room. It is 39x47 feet and the recreation room is 28 x 39 feet. These rooms are also used for the Lodge rooms of the Rebecca's and several small property and anti rooms. Work on the new building was to begin in the spring of that year. The old building was formerly the property of George V. Morris, who for years and up until 1880, conducted in it a general merchandising business. It is now occupied by Dr. J. J. Reynolds, Druggist (whom more will be written about later). The new building has from the year of 1902, always been one of the landmarks of the city.

The contract for tearing down the old building on the Oddfellow's lot and erecting a new three story block was given on May 15th, 1902, to Mr. Elliot Colliver of Carlisle, the contract price was close to $10,000. The material to be used on the outer walls was to be of pressed brick of the best grade. The work of tearing down the building was to begin the following week, and the main building later. The building was to be completed by November 15th, but the lower floors were to be ready for occupancy within ninety days. Dr. Reynolds moved his stock of drugs to the rooms of C. L. Dudley, then occupied by Hargis McDonald, and the room above it. Thomas H. Dudley, the Clothier, took the rooms then occupied by C. M. Putman, McDonald was to go to Lexington for a time and was to resume his business here in the fall. Mr. Putman's plans for the future was not given. Mr. McDonald was to give possession May 12th and Mr. Putman June 1st. Mr. Colliver, the contractor, was a former Fleming County man, formerly living at Sherburne.

The old Oddfellows building was built in the year of 1848-9 for Henry Bishop. The contractors for the brick work were James Eckles and Robert McCart, for the wood work was Joseph Warder, and for the plastering Martin P. Phillips. The firm of Bishop and Threlkeld had been doing business at the stand then occupied by the Langdon and Creasey Co. In the year of 1849, when they moved to the then new building the firm changed to Bishop & Morris, George Morris having married the daughter of Henry Bishop. The building remained in the Bishop and Morris family until 1881, when it was bought by the Oddfellows, their deed being dated May 23rd, 1881. On the first day of May, 1882, it was rented to Dr. John J. Reynolds, druggist, who moved to it from the same building that Bishop moved from. A further coincidence is the fact that the Oddfellows notified Dr. Reynolds to be ready to move on the first day of May, 1902, after just twenty years of occupancy. This room had but two tenants in fifty-three years. The other room, however, has had a number of tenants. The first tenant in it was A. Wallenstein, the Clothier, followed by LaRue and Son, Dry Goods, then James W. Singleton, Hardware, who was bought out by Roby and Son. They in turn were bought out by Andrews & Kackley. The next was Glascock & Taylor, Clothing. Succeeded by Glascock & Barksdale, then Thomas H. Dudley & Bro., then back to Thomas H. Dudley again, later to

125

T. H. & H. B. Dudley. It was a clothier for men, known now as The Men's Shop, owned by a group of local men.

The story of the Oddfellows building would not be complete without the name of Dr. J. J. Reynolds, one of Flemingsburg's most prominent and respected citizens. John J. Reynolds, one of our most energetic and enterprising business men, was born July 22nd, 1847, at Chambersburg, Pa. (A small town just out of Gettysburg a few miles). He was the third son of Dr. S. F. and Hannah Reynolds. His education was confined to the common schools of his native state until he arrived at the age of fourteen, when during the year of 1861, he entered the store of William Heyser at Chambersburg, Pa., as a clerk where he remained as a clerk until 1866. During that year he went to Philadelphia and attended the Philadelphia College of Pharmacy, graduating at that institution with honors in 1869. In 1870, he came to Kentucky and located in Louisville, where he was engaged as a clerk in the house of George Newman for a period of three years. He then returned to this native state of Pennsylvania, where he worked in the oil fields for three years. He then returned to Louisville and opened a drug store at the corner of Seventh and Walnut Streets in that city, in which he spent a term of three years. He then removed to the city of Atlanta, Georgia, where he became a member of the firm of Pemberton, Samuels & Reynolds, whoelsale and retail druggist. In 1881, he sold out his interest in this firm and located in Flemingsburg, Kentucky, and began business in the drug line in the room then known as the Teager building and was later the occupancy of the H. E. Landon Bluegrass Company. In May 1882, he moved into the then new Oddfellows Building on the corner of Main Cross and Water Streets, where he operated his drug store for so many years. The corner where his store stood was affectionately known as Reynold's Corner long after his death.

In November, 1877, he was married to Mrs. Antha Anderson, a daughter of the late Samuel E. Armstrong of Poplar Plains, Kentucky. To this union three children were born, of whom the eldest, a son, died at the age of ten.

126

Dr. Reynolds sustained the reputation as one of the most energetic and leading business men of our city. He was for years a member of the City Council and was a prime mover in the construction of the electric light plant in this city, which furnished the lights for Flemingsburg for years. He was zealous and an active member of the Christian Church, diligent, faithful and attentive to the matters of business, and eminently competent and reliable from a professional and business standpoint, strictly moral and upright, and a gentleman of irreproachable character and deportment. He won the confidence and esteem of the public, and built up a trade that made him prosperous and successful.

Dr. Reynolds was buried in the local cemetery in Flemingsburg, Kentucky. He has descendants now living in Fleming County (1967) that are land owners and business people of the highest type.

CHAPTER THIRTY-FOUR

FLEMING COUNTY'S MOST HORRIBLE
RAILROAD ACCIDENT — 1907

Double deck trestle of the C.F.&S. Railroad collapsed and entire train, engine, passenger coaches and freight cars plunge down thirty-eight feet, to the bottom of the trestle, carrying its entire crew and passengers to death or injury, with only a few that received a very light or no injury at all.

This is a story that only a few of Fleming County's senior citizens can now remember. It happened on Friday morning, May the 10th, 1907. The railroad known then as the C. F. & S., was a spur line that junctioned off the L. & N. at Johnson Junction about six miles west or northwest of Flemingsburg, Ky. and passed through our very modest and prosperous little town about one mile from town on the banks of Fleming Creek. It bore slightly to the left crossing the creek just a little ways up stream, from there it made its stop at Poplar Plains, a thriving little town six miles southeast of Flemingsburg. The sight of the old Depot at Poplar Plains, which set about one fourth mile east of the town, can still be seen. The site and the land around it now belongs to Mr. M. C. Colliver and his large holding of farm land. From there the very proud train (for its day) journeyed on its southeastern course, up small ravines, crossing small streams, slightly gaining in elevation on its five or six mile trip, coming out on the hilltop where one of the nicest towns in Fleming County stood and did a thriving business, the small city of Hillsboro, Ky. There was no Round House or turn table at Hillsboro, the train was driven into the station, it being the end of the line of the C. F. & S. Then the train was backed from there to its starting point at Johnson Junction. On this route which I have described to you, just out of Flemingsburg about half way between Flemingsburg and Poplar Plains, there the two deck trestle stood, thirty-eight feet high. There is much to write about this small railroad and all of the tales pro and con that have been told and written about it. I have pictures of this railroad and its trestle before the wreck, and the train and coaches after the wreck, and can well remember the engineer and his entire crew. Some of them lived to be old and useful citizens of Flemingsburg. I will try to condense their stories as I have heard them told many times, and also have other stories that were in the paper of that day, plus some pictures before and after the fatal wreck. First, I will give the engineer's own version of the wreck.

Engineer, Kirby Moore, Gives His Story of the Wreck

Engineer Moore gives a graphic description of the accident, how the trestle first gave way, and the frightful plunge to the bottom. He stated that several days before he had seen a dove that was building her nest in one of the joints of the trestle and every time he pulled on to the trestle that he would always look for her. He had watched her build her nest for days and the day before the wreck there were two eggs in it, so as the train pulled onto the trestle, he was looking down to see if the old dove was on her nest; then he saw one of the timbers sink down under the weight of the engine. He at once realized that it meant disaster and called at once to his fireman, Clarence Browning, to jump. Mr. Moore started out on the running board on his side, seeing in an instant that the engine was careening slightly to his side, he drew back and sat down on the seat with his feet on the outside of the window leading to the running board. He was in that position when the engine struck the ground. Fireman Browning was still in the cab with his head almost against the boilerhead. After pulling him away from the boiler, Mr. Moore went to the coach and with his bare hands tore away the splintered end of it, giving him a view of the inside.

In the corner was Miss Addie Newman, apparently lifeless, while near her was the Thomas baby, which was crying. Mr. Moore said this was all the life that was to be seen or heard in the wrecked coach at that time. Charles P. Duley, having gotten out on the other side, had gone to the branch to wash the blood from his eyes. Mr. Moore at once took Miss Addie Newman from the wreck and laid her on the grass thinking her dead. He next took from the wreck the Thomas baby. As soon as it was on the outside, it seemed to faint away and he thought it also dead. The third person to be taken out by Mr. Moore was a Mr. Thomas A. Fowles, who was badly cut about the head and was breathing with great difficulty. He laid the dying man on the grass and taking off his coat placed it under Mr. Fowles' head. About this time Mr. Chas. P. Duley, who had been up the track to call the section hands who responded quickly, came down the hill to join Mr. Moore. They then went to see about Clarence Browning and finding him sitting upon a big timber which had plunged in the cab of the engine, they took him out and laid him upon the grass and then proceeded to the relief of the other injured.

About this time Mr. Moore discovered that a fire had started among the freight in the wrecked box car which was between the engine and the coach. The fire had started in the end next to the engine, caused by a case of matches having been ignited by the fall. He at once took the coal scoop and dipped water from the wrecked tank and put the fire out, only to have it break out again in a short while, but the blaze was then put out for good without doing any harm. By this time, two colored section men arrived on the scene to aid in the work of rescue, and then a short time though it seemed ages, stated Mr. Moore, John F. Mills, an old Railroad man appeared on the banks above, and then the advance guard of relief. In a few minutes people came by the score, but by then all of the living victims had been taken out of the wreck. A large timber knocked off the whistle valve that soon emptied the boiler with steam and probably saved the life of Fireman Browning and maybe others.

Two deaths resulted from the horrible accident on the C. F. & S. R. R. of Friday, May the 10th, 1907. At the last trip this train made in its attempt to the town of Hillsboro, Ky., it never got beyond the ill-fated trestle that caved in at the cost of two lives and permanently injuring many more.

The trestle was built in the winter of 1878-9. The first regular trains being run over it in the spring of 1879. It was a double deck trestle, the lower deck being 20 feet and the upper 16 feet which with the stringers and ties made it 38 feet over all.

On the morning of May 10, 1907, when this train pulled out of its station with Hillsboro, Ky. its foremost stop on its line, it was already carrying a corpse of a man by the name of a Mr. Rankin. After making its usual stop at Flemingsburg from Johnson Station, it picked up several passengers as well as freight going to Popular Plains and Hillsboro, its other station. There were about 40 passengers and its usual crew. Most everyone seemed gay for the coming week-end, although it was raining a slow soft rain, and known only to God that the train was less than two miles from Fleming County's most noted tragedy, the fate of this train has already been described by its engineer, Kirby Moore.

According to the information that I have before me, the dead was Mr. Thomas Fowles, a timber dealer at Hillsboro, who died in about two hours without regaining consciousness, as was Mr. Harry Thomas, a barber, whose home was 1801 Eastern Avenue, Cincinnati, Ohio, who was killed instantly. Mr. Thomas and his wife were enroute to her home to attend the funeral of her father who lived at Hillsboro. When he left his Barber shop in Cincinnati, he had put a sign reading "Closed on account of death"; that sign remained there until after his own funeral. The injured were:

Clarence E. Browning — multiple fracture of left thigh, concussion of brain, scalds of neck, left ear and left hand, bruises over entire body. He is still unconscious after 48 hours. He is in plaster cast and late Wednesday Evening he made some move for the better, but is still very critical. His nurse at home is Miss Martin. Mr. Browning was the fireman on the ill-fated train.

Miss Addie Mae Newman, fracture, compound of right femur, limb has been adjusted in plaster cast, having an external wound makes her case a serious one. If it does not become septic, recovery is assured, but will be slow at best; also bruises on the body. Miss Boone is her nurse. She is at C. J. Sutton's home. Mrs. Harry Thomas, severe injury to kidney, cut on forehead that required several stitches, general bruises over the body, extremely nervous and suffering great pain, although her prorgess is satisfactory. She is at the Merchants Hotel.

Matt Bramble, the train's brakeman, fracture of right leg, cuts on the face, bruises over most of his body suffered profound shock, also injury to the spine. He is doing satisfactorily. J. D. Barnes is his nurse. He is at home.

Mrs. Myrtle Wheeler suffered from punctured wound of left jaw and broken right ankle, bruises are all over the body. She is at the Ryan's Hotel doing satisfactorily, with Miss Nellie Jones as her nurse.

Mrs. Lizzie Graham, fractured ribs and general bruises, also at Ryan's Hotel with Miss Nellie Jones as her nurse.

Miss Ethel Rawlings, two scalp wounds that required several stitches, several bruises over the body, doing well at home of J. M. Rawlings.

John Moore, dislocation of right shoulder, puncture wounds of the head and face. His body is badly bruised. He is at home.

Kirby Moore, the engineer of the ill fated train, severe bruises about the shoulders and face, but is able to go about.

C. P. Duley, the freight agent, two incised wounds of the scalp, cut on left hand, general bruises over the body. He is able to be out.

The baby Rankin's, cut on forehead and chin, nose broken and punctured wound of hand. At C. M. Lee's home.

The Thomas baby whose father was killed in the wreck

was taken to Falmouth, Ky., Tuesday, by his aunt, a Mrs. Held.

Orie Mannin was shaken up and dazed by the shock, but has now about recovered, was taken to his home in Hillsboro, Saturday.

The above reports on the people that were injured in the train wreck, are patients of Drs. Garr and Brice, both well-known physicians of Flemingsburg.

Drs. Robertson and Vice, also noted physicians of Flemingsburg, make their report on their patients that were injured in the wreck:

Mrs. Amelia Snodgrass, suffering from a severe scalp wound, profound shock of the brain and the spinal column, is now in a semi-conscious condition and shows signs of improvement. At the residence of J. W. Lawson.

Mrs. C. B. Rankin, suffering from three fractures and dislocated shoulder of the right arm, and fractures of the left arm just above the wrist. She is doing very well, sitting up some at the residence of Mrs. Susan Fant.

Mr. C. B. Rankin, severe bruises all over his body and limbs, has suffered severely but is now able to go about, at the Merchants Hotel.

Will B. Campbell, suffering from severe shock and bruises in the chest, is still coughing blood; his condition is still serious, but he has shown some improvement. He is at the Merchants Hotel.

Lan. Donaldson, one of Poplar Plains most noted colored men, also went down with the train to the bottom of the ravine, but came up hail and hearty, only minus one tooth.

Bruce Allen's Good Luck

Bruce Allen thinks that there is such a thing as a blessing in disguise. Some time ago he got a severe bruise on one of his legs which seemed to have affected the bone. It gave him a great deal of trouble, and some three weeks ago he gave up the place as brakeman on the C. F. & S. Railroad to Matt Bramble to have his leg operated on. He is now able to be out, almost well, while his substitute has been down to death's door.

133

Thousands View The Wreck

The wreck happened on Friday morning and the letters C. F. & S. stood for the Covington, Flemingsburg & Southern Railroad. By Friday evening and Saturday the news was well over Fleming County as well as other counties; crowds had begun to form from great distances; by Saturday evening the crowd was estimated to be at least two thousand or more, and by Sunday the crowd was estimated to be at least four thousand. Many of the spectators carried away pieces of the wrecked trestle or train for souvenirs.

Master mechanic, John F. Mills, and a force of men started in just a few days cleaning up the wreck and getting the engine ready to be pulled back on the track. They have it on its wheels on a temporary track laid up the side of the ravine and will soon be pulled up by a powerful block and tackle and put on the track to be brought to the shops here.

Engine No. 1

The engine is No. 1, the original engine, built by The Baldwin Locomotive Works of Philadelphia in January, 1877. It has almost been in constant use on the road since then. Train service resumed between here and Johnson Station, Saturday morning with Fred Singleton as engineer and Thomas H. Lee as conductor.

There was a collection taken up for the injured.

The collection that was taken up amounted to several thousand dollars for the injured, but when Mr. Bush, the general manager for the railroad, arrived here he asked for it to be returned to the owners, as the railroad would care for all people who were injured as well as to pay all of their expenses.

The telephone service was of great help.

As the news spread through the county aided by the splendid help of the telephone operators, which were Mrs. Bertie Kendall, Misses Elizabeth Kendall and Emma Lewis

134

Hopper. At that time the lights were turned off in the city at nine o'clock, but Mayor John Reynolds called on Messrs. Henderson and O'Bannon and asked that the electric lights burn all night until further notice, for both streets and dwellings which the owners were willing to cooperate.

Although this railroad never operated east of Flemingsburg again, it was put back in use and operated for many many years between Flemingsburg and Johnson Junction. Some of the crew went back to their old job, including the engineer, Kirby Moore, and worked for many years.

How the C. F. & S. Railroad Settled With Most of the Clients

It is understood that basis of settlement of all of the damage claims against the C. F. & S. R. R., growing out of the wreck of May 10, 1907, has been substantially agreed upon between the parties of interest and the matter may be finally signed up and settled today. The figures are understood to be about this way; Mrs. Amelia Snodgass, Mrs. Mary Thomas and Mrs. Nannie Rankin $1,500 each; estates of Harry Thomas and T. A. Fowles $1,200 each; C. B. Rankin, B. B. Snodgrass, Mrs. Sallie Graham, the Thomas baby and the Rankin baby a sum of $2,300, but could not get the exact figure of each one. Mrs. Wheeler $625, Will B. Campbell $175., estate of Miss Addie Newman $500., Miss Ethel Rawlings $350., Orie Manning $25., and Lan. Donaldson before mentioned, $25 for loss of tooth. In the matter of Matt. Bramble no settlement was made as the company claims that he was settled with in full and that they have his receipt full, properly signed and witnessed. This wreck of the C. F. & S. R. R. at the time covered the front pages of many newspapers for miles around. It was almost impossible to write the story as it appeared on the pages at the time, so in my poor way I have tried to condense it, and to apply it according to the records.

CHAPTER THIRTY-FIVE

THE RISE AND FALL OF FLEMING COUNTY'S
JUDGE C. E. BOOE

Judge Booe's air castle of dreams collapsed on Nov. 21, 1908. Charges of forgery and shortage made against auditor's clerk, C. E. Booe, former judge of Fleming County. Shortage many thought to run between $40,000 and $50,000. If this writer should attempt to write all the stories, pro and con on the fantastic life of Judge Booe, it would make an interesting book by itself; from records, old newspapers from Frankfort, Louisville, Lexington and some newspapers that have no heading comes the story of this man.

The records speak of his wife, a daughter and son. Judge Booe came from Covington, Ind. in 1888, having been married but a short time to Miss Kate Nute, daughter of Captain Charles Nute of Mt. Carmel, a prominent family of that community. He and his brother-in-law, Charles Nute, went into the furniture and undertaking business and for some years they also operated the Merchants Hotel, which at that time stood where the Farmers Deposit Bank now stands. Judge Booe was a man of pleasant manner and made friends rapidly. He seemed to have a golden touch with whoever he came in contact with and was therefore a gifted politician, of which he plied his trade well. He was a member of the Democratic party. The story is told that as Judge Booe was on the train from Johnson Junction to Flemingsburg, he conversed with a man from Flemingsburg and when he was told that Fleming County was a Democratic County, Judge Booe decided then to become a Democrat.

In 1892, he was elected by the Board of Magistrates as County Judge succeeding to the unexpired term of the then Judge J. P. Harbeson, who resigned to take the place of Circuit Judge. Judge Booe was afterwards elected, and then re-elected, resigning in August, 1900 to take the place of Claim Clerk in the Auditor's office at Frankfort under Gus G. Coulter.

When S. W. Hager succeeded to the Auditor's office in 1904, Judge Booe was made assistant auditor but still left in charge of the claims desk. When the new Republican administration came in they wanted a man who was familiar with the work of the office and they retained Judge Booe, who was very popular and highly esteemed by everyone whom had ever once come in contact with him, regardless of their politics, and he remained there until his house of cards fell in on Nov. 21, 1908.

Few men have ever lived in Fleming County that had more friends than Judge Booe. They loved him for his jolly ways and he was almost always the very first to come to a friend with aid when he was in trouble. When he would come back to Fleming County from Frankfort, on a visit, everyone was delighted to see him, all was glad to know that he was prospering and no one for a moment suspected him of wrong doing. His wife and daughter, then a young woman, a son then about 8 years of age, were all very popular through the county and liked by all who knew them, and the deepest sympathy was felt for them whose life was clouded by the sad end to the career of their father.

The fast life of Frankfort official circles of that day seems to have been too much for Judge Booe. Speculations on the Board of Trade by margin was followed by betting on the horses at Louisville, Latonia as well as other vices. So in order to get the money to keep up the pace for the things that he loved so well, he began to embezzle State funds, which brought disgrace on himself and his entire family.

The Louisville Herald had the following article probably written by a young man of Flemingsburg, C. Woodson Dudley, which is headed, "The Pity Of It All." "He was a man beloved by all that knew him, generous, kindly, fond of little children, and with a kindly word for those that he met on life's highways. In the church where he had occupied his seat for years, he was honored and respected in the religious and philanthropic organizations to which he belonged. He was regarded as a man to be counted on for wise advice and practical help. In the public office that he held, he was trusted as one beyond reproach or suspicion. Then the gambling germ crept into his blood. The lure of stocks and race tracks with their possibilities of easy money appealed to that latent speculative propensity which every man with red blood in his arteries has felt. He tried a flier in the market, he backed a sure thing at Latonia or Churchill Downs, he won; he played the game of chance again, he lost; so fortune fluctuated. Money, trust money, was passing through his hands; it was a simple matter to borrow with very good intention of returning; he borrowed, he won, he repaid; he borrowed again and lost. Further losses followed, the borrowing became speculations, desperate grasping without consideration of the future, only the motive of self-protection compelling to avert immediate disaster — at last exposure comes. The nightmare is at an end — the hidous reality of disgrace confronts him. Oh! the pity of it all. All the past of happiness in the trust and honor of friends and public vanishes like a beautiful dream. The reputation of years are gone, the admirable manhood that people have loved is a desolate ruin. Can you wonder there are men who oppose the race track and bucket shop?"

The Fleming Gazette, Tuesday, December 1, 1908
"A close friend of Judge Booe's as well as adviser here in Fleming County, had this to say of the Judge: 'The money that Booe absconded was spent chiefly in living expenses, while he speculated some and played the horses, too. His losses along these lines were not extensive, but he always was a hale-fellow-well-met, and spent his money lavishly for one of his means and circumstances. A friend or acquaintance of Judge Booe's hardly ever met him in Frankfort but what the always genial Judge returned his greeting with 'First rate, I thank you' and then proceeded to show courtesy or attention which frequently cost money.

138

He was a generous giver for church or other charitable purposes, and when it came to campaign contributions, Judge Booe always astonished the campaign managers with his generosity. Only a year ago it told of him on returning from Flemingsburg to Frankfort, he tossed a large sum of money to a party worker at Johnson Junction and urged that every thing possible be done for the election of his party's ticket.

"In speaking of his present plight, Judge Booe is said to offer no excuse for his dishonesty more than to say he simply took the money to spend on his friends and to live well, and that he was unable to resist the temptation. Most everyone in Fleming County knew Judge Booe, nearly everyone liked him for his genial manner and clever disposition, and the news of his exposure came as a surprise and cause of regret to most people. His family has always been highly esteemed and his present position is a sad and heavy blow to them.

"How Judge Booe, with all the luxuries and frivolities of the life he has been living, could enjoy such an existence when he could not but realize the exposure and disgrace sure to follow, we can not understand. His speculations were so bold and daring that he surely realized an accounting would come, and that not only himself, but his loved ones were certain to share in his ultimate shame. Nevertheless, such men always have been or probably always will be. The only explanation for such a life is that there is a streak of character which might be akin to the kleptomaniac."

This is the headlines of a Frankfort newspaper on the morning of Nov. 21, 1908. Special dispatch to the Herald: "Charges of forgery and shortage made against Auditor's Clerk, Charles E. Booe. Friends of Claim Clerk take poison and pistol from him in fear that he might end his life after Auditor F. P. James accuses him of shortage — arrested on warrant and released on $5,000 bond, on application of most prominent men of Frankfort and pastor of his church. Thought that the shortage may run near $50,000.

"Judge Booe had a mania for high living and big time gambling which few, if any, of his friends, ever thought entered his mind. This coupled with the race tracks has led C. E. Booe, once the very popular County Judge of Fleming County, Ky., to the penitentiary charged with misappropriation of the States funds and with forgery. Judge Booe, assistant auditor under S. W. Hager and at present Claims Clerk in the office of Auditor Frank P. James, was arrested in his home here tonight and later released on bond in the amount of $5,000 furnished by the following men: J. W. Gale, E. M. Wallace, A. H. McClure, Rev. C. R. Hudson and Judge J. H. Hazelrigg." The shock occasioned by the discovery of Judge Booe's alleged shortage shook the Capital City to its very foundations, and close upon its heels came another sensation, when it was learned that Judge Booe, soon after being confronted with evidence upon which the charges were made against him, purchased a quantity of arsenic at a local drug store. Later when the druggist heard about Booe's shortage with the State Auditor's office, some of Booe's friends called on him and took the poison and also a pistol off of his person in fear that he might commit suicide.

"Judge Booe is charged among other things with padding vouchers for claims against the State. When confronted with his alleged irregulations this afternoon, he at first declared that he was guilty only on clerical errors, but during the course of his examination by the State Treasurer Farley, Auditor James and Inspector Thatcher, he became greatly aggitated and offered to reimburse the State in the amount of $850, the shortage he was charged with during the month of January, 1908 and he offered to deposit with the Auditor, stock in the Capitol Trust Co. valued at $5,000 for the latter's own protection. It is said that later Judge Booe told his wife and friends that his affairs were badly involved. For several days Judge Booe's department in the Auditor's office had been undergoing a quiet investigation by the State Inspector and the Auditor. Most of the work was done at the noon hour, or when Judge Booe

140

was absent from the office, and when sufficient evidence was secured to make out a case aganist him, he was confronted with it. This morning he was asked to step over to Treasurer Farley's office, and there in the presence of the Treasurer, Auditor James and State Inspector Thatcher, he was asked to explain why certain checks drawn by the treasurer from claims against the State did not correspond with the vouchers in the Auditor's office, from which amount the checks were computed, Judge Booe is said to have declared that he was guilty of clerical error and that he could not explain the discrepancies at the time. Other sets of checks and papers were handed to him with the request for an explanation that he could not explain. He was greatly aggitated during the questioning of the treasurer and the Auditor and great beads of perspiration gathered on his forehead. It was said that he finally stated to the Treasurer that he did not want any one to suffer by an error that he had made and said 'It looks like I have made a blunder, but I am willing to make good the money, if that will satisfy you gentlemen'."

"Judge Booe was told to go to his lunch and to return to the Auditor's office, when he would be given more papers to look over. He returned about two o'clock, but in the meantime Auditor James, Inspector Thatcher and others had gone over to the Court house, where the Auditor secured an attachment, in order to protect himself from loss as best he could because of alleged irregularities on the part of Judge Booe . . ."

How Suspicions Were Aroused For Judge Charles E. Booe

The irregularities charge against Judge Booe were discovered by the merest accident a few days ago before the discovery of his shortage. A State official was standing on a street corner in conversation with a local merchant, when the most popular and genial Judge Booe came by, with his usual hearty greeting of, "First rate, and how are you fine gentlemen?" So after a short conversation, the Judge went on and the merchant with no suspicion on his part remarked to the State official that it was strange that Judge Booe cashed so many State checks with the merchants of the city instead of using the banks. Not showing any alarm the State official inquired how many have you cashed. "Oh, several hundred of them in the past year or so," replied the merchant, "and maybe three or four thousand during the past several years. The Judge was in my store a day or two ago and I obliged him as usual."

The official passed lightly over the subject, but when he reached his office, he fell to thinking what possible exiguous reason would cause Judge Booe to cash checks made out to the State Treasurer at local stores. He began an investigation, visiting several of the banks and examining checks, many which bore Judge Booe's endorsement and others which did not. Then he examined canceled checks among the State Treasurer's files and found that many of them prior to 1908 bore the same endorsement under the endorsement of the one to whom the check was originally made out. In going over papers in the Auditor's office the official discovered that most of the checks had been made out with others in the settlement of claims against the Commonwealth, many of which were paid at the time of the Sheriff's settlements with the Auditor. A conference of the officials was called at once and some of the checks were traced directly to Judge Booe, who had cashed them either at the store of local merchants or at the banks.

When taken before Judge Polsgrove after the warrant had been sworn out, Booe's bond was fixed at $10,000. His friends, however, asked for it to be reduced, and it was later set at $5,000. He was not taken to jail, but was under the surveillance of his friends.

Judge Booe is known as a chronic stock gambler and a better on the races. It is said in Frankfort that every morning he would call up his brokers in Louisville and place his bets. On the other hand, in his private life here, Judge Booe is favourably known. He has been for several years an elder in the First Christian Church here and passed the contribution plate on Sundays. He is exalted ruler of

142

the Frankfort Y.M.C.A. and prominent in every phase of civic life during the eight years that he has lived here. When Auditor James first discussed this matter with Judge Booe, the judge, at first excused to leave James' office, hurried to his own office, and papers that he had hidden in three different places were gathered up and hurriedly burned.

Public Turned Against Judge Booe

"The Judge has given several reasons why he stole money from the State Auditor's office but none is a good excuse. (Salary was reduced).

"Judge Booe's salary as assistant Auditor under Hagar was $2,000. When Auditor James decided to retain him in office he was placed in charge of the claims desk and his salary was reduced to $1,500, according to one of the auditor's clerks. Judge deplored this cut in his compensation and stated that he would have to make up the difference in some way. When asked what method he proposed to pursue, he was said to have replied, 'Well, I've been pretty lucky in the stock market and I guess I'll have to play the game for higher stakes now.' From his arm chair at home, Judge Booe tells how he first took money. 'Avoid temptation,' is his warning to all. Stole because he was prompted by subtle tempter, stole when he didn't need the money, stole because he did need the money, had an urge to steal, had an urge to gamble, had an urge to donate money for churches, lodges, politics, loved to spend money that he couldn't afford on his own friends and his friends were many, lust for stealing 'I couldn't help it, I had no motive other than I did not have the strength to resist the temptation that sprung into my mind.' When asked if any one else was mixed up in this with him, his reply was this, 'As God as my judge,' said Judge Booe, 'there is not another soul in this world that knew about it but myself. I did it all myself and, if there is any one else under suspicion or accused, it is wrong. No one had any idea that I was taking the money, and if you have any one else under suspicion go and release them at once.' "

Didn't Fear Exposure

"The thought of being caught never entered my mind. While I did not take the first money as an experiment, but because I could not help it, the thought of being trapped never entered my mind. When I was caught I did not know what to do, I was dazed and puzzled, and it is true that I had made up my mind at that time to commit suicide. I left the State House with the intention of getting prussic acid for I had heard that it was certain to kill. I was refused the poison and bought the arsenic. I did not want arsenic, for I had been told that it did not work well, for if too much was taken it would make one sick, but would not kill. I intended to use arsenic, however, but I was prevented from doing so, and have now made up my mind that I will not commit suicide. I am going to plead guilty when my trial comes up." The pointed question was asked, "Was there ever any member of your family insane? Judge seemed to resent all questions about his family and insanity. "Now I want to tell you that I am not insane, I am as sane as I was then and as sane then as I am now. I did not take the money because I was insane, but because I could not help it. I guess I wanted it, although I did not need it and never have needed it." Judge Booe was then asked what he did with the money and nis reply was, "You have asked what I did with the money and I will have to tell you that I do not know. I put it with my other money and used it, I did not hoard it up with the expectation of using it in a race for Auditor or for any other purpose. I merely took it and invested it with my other money and spent it with my other money. I have turned over to my attorney about $10,000 worth of securities and they will be used to pay back the money as far as it will go. It is every cent that I have in the world."

The Times Special Service, Frankfort, Ky., Nov. 27, 1908

Judge C. E. Booe, waves examining trial before County Judge J. H. Polsgrove this morning and was held to await the action of the grand jury. His bond was fixed at $5,000 and bail was immediately given. Judge Booe appeared in court accompanied by his attorney, Judge Hazelrigg. Judge Booe will plead guilty on all thirty-five counts, each charging a felony.

Judge Booe tells when embezzlement first entered his mind: "There were a number of us clerks sitting around, talking about the money that had been taken by a clerk under Auditor Sam Stone. I was not familiar with the circumstances and asked some questions about it. The explanation was that he had taken claims out of the batch of vouchers and put them in another, and then drawn a check in favor of himself. No sooner had this explanation been made to me than there flashed through my mind like a flash of lightning why should he have done that? It would have been easier for him to have raised the claims and there would have been less chance of getting caught. This thought preyed on my mind day and night, and no matter where I went or what I did, it was constantly there. Although I tried hard to throw it off, it constantly stayed with me. There seemed to be an irresistible something, I know not what to call it, that seemed to force me by degrees until I weakened and, finally, decided to try my plan. I tried it and it was successful. I did not need the money and I will never be able to tell why I did it except that I could not help myself. I tried the plan again for another amount and again it worked, so then I was so sure that my plan was perfect that I never had the least bit of fear that it would ever be known."

"If I had gotten all the money in the State," he said, "It would not have compensated me, for the torture I have suffered since I have been caught. No one will ever know how I have suffered, so my advice is to resist temptation, fight it off even if a position or greater sacrifices have to be made."

Judge Booe was indicted on January 5, 1909 by the Franklin Grand Jury on the 35 counts, each charging a felony in the Department of the Auditor of Public Accounts and a bench warrant for him was issued at once by Judge

Stout, and his bond was raised from $5,000 to $10,000 which he was unable to raise and the judge was asked by State officials and other prominent people to lower his bond to the original $5,000, which was done and Judge Booe was allowed to go home until his trial.

Frankfort, Kentucky — January 8, 1909

"Judge Booe sentenced to five years in State prison. Former Auditor's Clerk pleads guilty on first count of forgery — Begins to serve his sentence. Affecting scenes at home and the court room, Judge Stout grants a continuance on other thirty-four indictments.

"Judge Booe, one time assistant State Auditor, tonight began a five year sentence behind the wall of the State Penitentiary here. Judge Booe was sentenced in the Frankfort Circuit Court this afternoon by Judge Robert L. Stout on a count of forgery, pleading guilty to one of thirty-five indictments returned against him by the Commonwealth. The other indictments returned against him on the plea of the counsel were continued until the April term of the court. Judge Booe was not taken immediately to the prison, but allowed to return to his home under guard of a deputy sheriff and to eat dinner with his wife and his young son.

"Judge Booe was a very large man, and Warden Warner Mudd had an extra large size suit of stripes made for him as there was none in the prison large enough for him. Judge Booe appeared in the Penitentiary today garbed in a nice fitting suit of prison stripes that was made to his special measure last Tuesday. The prison tailor had nothing in the regular size that would fit the new prisoner. He was assigned to work in the clothing department but this may be only temporary. He occupies cell No. 30."

After going through hundreds of old papers and other records, I have no more news about Judge Booe. I, too, am wondering what became of the other thirty-four counts against him, and if he served the five years and what became of him, his wife and two children. Maybe through records in Frankfort some facts could be discovered.

CHAPTER THIRTY-SIX

AVENGED AT THE STAKE

This chapter is composed of stories covering the period from 1899 to 1920, with all starting by breaking the law and ending the same way, which today would probably be handled altogether in a different way.

This sad and unhappy story happened in Mason County which is the Mother County of Fleming. The true names in this story are not being used, but the story is quoted from other records that I have in my collection of Fleming County and other sections of this part of Kentucky.

Oct. 5th, 1899

One of the most foul and atrocious murders that has ever disgraced our State occurred on the L. & N. Railroad near Lewisburg last Thursday afternoon. Mrs. John Ashboro was brutally murdered by a Negro named Rick Cole, and was found lying in a cabin near her own home with her throat cut and her skull crushed in.

The first news of the terrible affair came here about 7 o'clock Thursday evening, in the shape of a telephone message to I. M. Ashboro, who is a relative of the unfortunate woman.

The murdered woman was about 40 years old and lived with her husband on the farm where she was killed. Her maiden name was Miss Maud Lang. The poor woman was buried at the family burying ground Friday. After services had been held over the remains, the black fiend who committed the crime was arrested shortly afterwards, and made the following confession: My name is Rick Cole, am about twenty years old, was born at Germantown, but went to live with Eldwood Tolle when small with whom I lived for six years. Since then have been around different places up to a year ago, when I went to live with Mr. John Ashboro. My business was to do the kitchen work, including the cooking. Relate the circumstances from the time of the return of Mrs. Ashboro from Maysville, he was asked.

"At I o'clock Mrs. Ashboro returned from town. I went to the buggy to help her to carry in her purchases. When we had gotten to the house she was telling of the things that she had purchased and among them she showed me her new hat and asked me how I liked it. She then told the arrangements to make soap; as she was going to Cincinnati next week for a visit. She handed me a pan of meat scraps to take to my cabin and she was to follow me and to tell me how to make the soap. I went in the lead, we got to the cabin and went into my room, which contained the usual furniture, then I stepped behind her and locked the door. Mrs. Ashboro said, "Rick, what did you do that for?" I said, "Oh, nothing." I picked up a stick as big around as my thumb and hit her over the left temple, as she began to fall I caught her in my arms, pressed my hand over her mouth, as she was screaming, then laid her on the bed. After that I went out, strolled around the cabin grounds, and came back. I heard her groaning. I did not want her to suffer. I then went to the kitchen and got my razor out of my coat pocket and came back to the cabin and cut her throat twice. Then I went into the yard and in about a half hour I came back to the cabin and found her still alive; then I went out and got the ax, came back in and hit her twice in the head. I then locked the cabin door and threw the key away. While I was in the cabin, Bill Wright, a young colored fellow that works at Moore's, came over to see me. I saw him but did not want him to see me. He walked around the yard for a while and then walked away. I came out of the cabin and yelled at him. He came back and said, "Where were you, Rick?" I replied, "I was in the orchard." "What is the matter around here?" he asked. I said, "Nothing," but he said, "What is all of that blood about? Yes, you do know, and you were here, for I saw your checkered shirt through the cabin window. Come with me and we will look in the cabin window." I went with him. "Why, there is something the matter, what is to be done?" I said. He said, "Let's ring the farm bell." We rang the bell and saw Mr. Ashboro in the field, but he did not come. Ross said that he would go after him. I said, "I will go." and did. Mr. Ashboro and four farm hands came back. "How did you break the news to Mr. Ashboro?" "I was asked. I told him that I had just come home from Lewisburg getting the mail, and that I could not find Mrs. Ashboro anywhere, and that there was blood all around the cabin, and that the cabin door was locked. He said, "Rick, you are fooling." He came and kicked the cabin door open and discovered things as I have related.

He sent men around the neighborhood to inform the neighbors of the crime. When asked the consequences that follows, committing such an act, I replied, seriously, "They will hang me. I had no motive in committing the crime, for Mrs. Maud was always good and kind to me."

Rick Cole was arrested and lodged in jail in Maysville and excitement was so high Thursday night it was thought he would be lynched before daybreak. Such was not the case, although a large crowd was threating around the jail all night. There seemed to be no leader to the mob which was an unorganized crowd of men and boys.

On the following day Cole was given a preliminary hearing at the jail before Judge Newell and was committed without bail to answer for his crime at the coming term of the November Court. He was then put on the C. & O. train and taken to Covington for safe keeping.

Rick Cole Pays An Awful Penalty
December 6th, 1899

One of the most horrible tragedies that ever occurred in a civilized community took place in Maysville last Wednesday, when Rick Cole, the rape and murder fiend, was taken by a mob and burned at the stake. The brute's eyes were poked out with pointed sticks, cayenne pepper and vitriol were poured in the sockets. He was slashed with knives and beaten with clubs, and finally lashed to a tree and was roasted to death. The members of the mob were wild in their frenzy and mad in their thirst for revenge; but the brutal and horrible nature of the whole affair was more than equal by the fiendish and vicious crime of which Cole had confessed of being guilty — the assault and murder of Mrs. Ashboro, the full particulars of which are too horrible to relate.

This lynching all took place in broad daylight in the presence of hundreds of people. The mob was led by John Ashboro, the husband of the murdered woman. There was no effort to conceal the identity of those who participated in the affair and after it was all over, Mr. Ashboro declared that he would sleep better that night than any since the fatal day when he returned to his home to find his loving wife ravished and murdered and sweltering in her own blood.

Although the participants in the mob were well-known, it is thought no prosecutions will result, as public sentiment is too strongly opposed to such a course.

When Cole was brought to Maysville it was thought by the authorities that the law would be allowed to take its course, as Judge Harbeson had been assured by relations of Mr. Ashboro that he would not attempt to deal out summary punishment. For this reason the State Militia was not asked for, and it is reasonably certain that Cole would have been hanged according to law.

The excitement was so great over the affair that court was adjourned by Judge Harbeson until the following Monday. We think this moral as taken from the Maysville Ledger should be especially worthy of consideration: "It was an awful thing to see such wracked upon a human being, but when you know that inside of thirty-five years there have been a hundred murders committed in Mason County, and not a single murderer has been hung, when you know that a few dollars, a slick lawyer and a jury of ignoramuses are all that is necessary to acquit any bloody-handed villain; when you know these things, how can you blame people

150

for seeking that protection (be they black or white) which the courts have so long denied."

The Clipping, From An Unknown Newspaper

The horrible exhibition of cruelty at Maysville, Kentucky last week should be an impressive lesson to those who are responsible for the laxity of the laws in the punishment of crime. Hundreds of murders are being committed in the State every year, and very rarely is it indeed that the guilty are punished on the gallows. The responsibility for this state of affairs rests partly with the courts and partly with those who constitute the juries. Changes of venue, postponements of trials, the right of appeal, legal technicalities, etc., and chicken-hearted jurors have the means of setting free thousands of persons guilty of murder in the first degree.

(So writes an unknown reporter for an unknown newspaper. As the writer of this story, I have only written what has already been written before).

CHAPTER THIRTY-SEVEN

HUSBAND'S IRE

A husband's ire leads to the shooting of his wife and her escort only to be murdered 39 days later. As I put this undying story together, that came to a climax on July 29, 1908, but started a few years before, I have the clippings of an unidentified newspaper which carried this story on the front page at the time. I have also interviewed people at this writing that were eye witnesses at the time, July 29th, 1908. The names of the family that were involved in this story are fictitious, but the story is true. I will write the story of the shooting of Mrs. Fred Shaw, by her husband, Fred Shaw.

An exciting tragedy was enacted Wednesday night about 8:30 o'clock in front of W. L. Wilson's home on Kalamont, in which Mrs. Fred Shaw, nee Miss Betty Brown, was shot through the calf of her lower right limb and John Mauck was shot four times in the lower limb, all the wounds being flesh wounds and not considered dangerous. The parties that were shot claim that Fred Shaw, husband of the first named was the pistol user.

It seems that Mauck and Mrs. Shaw were together walking west on the pavement and, at a point between the yards of W. L. Wilson and S. L. Hetherington, someone approached them from the rear and began firing. Three shots were fired in rapid succession and after a short interval two more. The woman ran towards the veranda of Mr. Hetherington and fell on the steps; Mauck ran to near the house and fell.

Several people quickly gathered and taking charge of the two wounded people removed them to their homes. Immediately after the shooting, two men ran from the scene, crossing the street in front of the residence of W. M. Wilt and passing down the cut-off street leading to Mt. Sterling Pike a third was said to have run and jumped over into the

Glascock field, which if true, would make three of the party involved in the attack.

Shaw and his wife had been married about four years and have one child. They have had much trouble and were not living together. The day of the shooting she had him arrested and tried on a charge of failure to support and he was held under bond of $150 for the grand jury. At the close of the trial, an exciting scene was witnessed at the court house, when she attacked one of the witnesses.

John Mauck is a married man and father of two children living in Lexington and has been here several weeks working at the carpenter trade and visiting his father and friends of this city.

Thursday morning Shaw came in and admitted to the shooting. He went before Judge Sousley in the afternoon and was placed under bond of $500, to appear before the grand jury.

Killed By Wife

Fred Shaw was laid low by bullets from a pistol in the hands of his wife. Yesterday morning about 8:45 o'clock, Mrs. Betty Brown Shaw shot and killed her husband, Fred Shaw, at the depot here in the presence of quite a crowd of people who were awaiting departure of the train. The date was Monday morning, September 7th, 1908. The scene took place at the ticket window, in the waiting room at the C. F. & S. R. R. in this city, just before the departure of the 8:45 train. Mrs. Betty Shaw fired four shots from a .38 caliber revolver at her husband, Fred Shaw, two of them taking effect and causing his death almost instantly. (To bring you closer to the scene, I will mix the headlines of the tragedy of several paper clippings that I have).

One morning, a short time before train time, Mrs. Shaw walked to the waiting room of the depot and took her seat, the third seat from the end of the seat next to the ticket window. She carried a small hand bag in which it is said that she carried the fatal weapon. Just how long she had been there no one could say, but about 8:40, Fred Shaw

153

walked in to buy a ticket to Maysville, being on his way to a fair at some point in Ohio. There were probably fifteen people in the waiting room at the time, and it seemed that Shaw was not aware of his wife's presence there until he was near the ticket window. As he pulled a large roll of money that was estimated by some witnesses to be as much as $500, he laid a two-dollar bill in the window to pay for his fare, and just as George Faulkner, the ticket agent, was in the act of unlocking the cash drawer to get the change, Mrs. Shaw from her seat fired the first shot — the muzzle of the gun not being over two feet from the doomed man. The ball struck about six inches below the right shoulder and ranged slightly upward. Almost instantly the second shot followed, this one missed the mark and took effect in the right breast of Shaw and passed through the region of the heart, and soon afterwards, was taken out from under the skin on the left side. A third shot was fired, but it was never learned whatever became of the ball.

As the shooting started, the roll of money that was in Shaw's hand dropped to the floor and as he slowly crumpled to the floor, with eyes of hatred on his wife, at the same time he was trying desperately to draw his own .38 revolver from his pocket. He died almost instantly in his tracks, and as Betty Shaw passed beside the dead body of her husband, it was said by witnesses that she stooped down and picked up the roll of money, before passing through the door that led outside.

As she reached the door, someone said, "You have killed Fred Shaw." She replied, in a cool, firm tone, "Yes, I killed him." She then walked to the end of the platform placing the pistol, pointing downward against her left breast, she fired the remaining load. The ball seemed to have been deflected from its course as it struck a locket and chain that she wore around her neck. It did not enter her breast but took effect in the fleshy part of her upper left arm and came out just above the elbow. She then walked down the pavement, her empty pistol swinging from the right hand, until she met John Cummins at a point just below the store of James W. Overley. When Mr. Cummins noticed that her shirt waist was on fire, he stopped her and extinguished the blaze and walked to her home with her.

The facts leading up to this tragedy or following, some five years ago. After the return of Fred Shaw, after serving several years in the U.S. Army in the Philippine Islands, they were married. Family difficulties arose and they separated, but afterwards went together, living in Connersville, Indiana. When he again abandoned her, Mrs. Shaw returned to the home of her parents of this city. Later, Fred Shaw came back and trouble ensued between them. At one time it was reported that Mrs. Shaw had chased her husband on the streets with a pistol with the avowed intention of killing him.

Still later, a reconciliation took place, followed by another rapture. She then had him arrested for non-support of their child and he was held on bond to the Circuit Court on this charge. Shortly after this, on the night of July 29th it was alleged that Fred Shaw shot his wife in the leg, that has already been related in this story.

As may naturally be supposed, there was a scene of wild confusion in that little depot waiting room at the C. F. & S. Railroad office when the shooting began — ladies screamed and rushed for the windows, some going out one way and some another, and it is almost a miracle that nobody caught one of the stray bullets. The ball which wounded Mrs. Shaw in some mysterious way rebounded from the concrete floor of the walk and was caught in the coat-tail pocket of Thomas L. Givon who was standing near by.

Soon after the tragedy, Mrs. Shaw was put under arrest and under guard. Her examining trial was first set for Tuesday afternoon, and later, was set for Thursday at 9 o'clock, but on Wednesday morning Mrs. Shaw went before Judge Sousley and waived examining trial, and was ordered to Maysville jail to await October court. Sheriff John Will Goddard took her down Wednesday afternoon and delivered her to the jailer of Mason County.

A clipping from a newspaper in Connersville, Ind., has

this to say about Mr. and Mrs. Fred Shaw who had been living in that city. The paper says that Fred Shaw is missing from here having sold his household goods and left while his wife and babe was on a visit to her parents in Kentucky. Mrs. Shaw returned to Connersville several days ago and could not find any trace of her missing husband. Another family was living in the house that they had occupied.

When Mrs. Betty Brown Shaw was brought back from Maysville to Flemingsburg to face the grand jury for the murder of her husband, Fred Shaw, she related to the jury all the hardships that she had while living with him. She told the jury many a sad story of their life, and that she had to flee on several occasions with their young son in her arms to save their lives; how she had tried to preserve their marriage, but it seemed that all was lost, and on several occasions he had threatened to kill her, and that she had found out that he was leaving the next morning for some town in another state, but she knew not where. She was determined to find out, so she went to the depot the next morning to try and coax him not to go, that she and their son both needed him. She had discovered early that morning that he had taken all the money that they had in the world; so her plan was to go to the depot and have a talk with him. The gun which she was carrying in her handbag was for protection, as he had threatened her on several occasions.

She admitted that she had gone early to the depot and had stood outside for some time hoping that he would come by so that she could talk to him without anyone knowing anything about their troubles, but at last she grew tired and went inside to get a seat. In a short time her husband came in. As he was in the process of buying a ticket, she thought that he saw her and that he so quickly went for his gun that he dropped the roll of money on the floor. In order to save her own life, she at once drew her gun from out of the handbag that she was carrying and fired point blank at him at a close range. She thought that the first shot had missed and he was still trying to get his gun from his pocket, so she then fired the second shot that missed, but in rapid succession she fired three or four shots. When questioned about trying to take her own life, she remarked that she would rather die than live. After Mrs. Shaw had been on the witness stand before the grand jury for most of a full day, the grand jury considered her case for some time and voted to not indict her — that she acted in the defense of her own life.

The Funeral of Fred Shaw

The funeral of Fred Shaw was set for the next Wednesday after the killing, but was postponed until Thursday on account of the examining trial of his wife, Mrs. Betty Brown Shaw who is accused of the murder, and later, was postponed until Saturday so that a brother and sister, who were living in Montana may have time to attend the funeral of their brother.

This is a headline from the Ledger, Maysville, Ky.:

Taken To Maysville

Mrs. Betty Brown Shaw of Flemingsburg, who shot and killed her husband there on the 7th of September, was taken before Judge Sousley Wednesday morning and waived examining trial and will likely be indicted before the October grand jury. Due to the condition of the jail in Flemingsburg, which is devoid of a woman's department, the court in Flemingsburg ordered the prisoner to be taken to the jail in Maysville which was done. Sheriff Goddard went with her on the 12:45 train Wednesday. Noting her arrival in that city, The Ledger says: The noted prisoner arrived here over the L. & N. about four o'clock yesterday and her presence as she walked from the depot west on Third Street to the jail, flanked on either side by Sheriff Mackey and policeman Crawford, created a decided sensation.

Mrs. Shaw has extremely clear cut features and was considered to be one of the most beautiful women in this part of the state. She was attired in a suit of mourning, as her husband lay dead seventeen miles away in Flemingsburg, at the works of her own hands. She had a stately mind and bearing as she passed along the thoroughfare, seemingly oblivous to her surroundings and the gaze and the stare of every one present. With her eyes set straight ahead, never once did she ever cast a glance to the right, neither to the left, but went forward apparently lost to earthly things. She does not appear as one who would commit a murder without a grievance impelling her to the act; but be that as it may, in taking the life of her husband, she has jeopardized her own.

* * * *

This is to give you more about the lives of the people who go to make this sad but true story. At the time of this murder, Fred Shaw was 34 years old and his wife, Betty Brown Shaw was 26 years old. Both had been raised in Fleming County, as their parents before them, and all were prominent and respected people of that day. For some reason or other Fred Shaw had a lust to wander, rarely did his people ever know where he was. He roamed throughout the West at will, coming home at long intervals, but for some reason known only to himself he had enlisted in the U.S. Army to go to the Philippine Islands.

Fred Shaw was a noted gambler, but like most gamblers — rich today and broke tomorrow. The tales of his gambling ability are still being told and re-told around our county by the older citizens here. It is said that in cards he could deal so fantastic that he could deal from a deck of cards any card that he wanted; for the game of dice (commonly known as craps), he was equally as good or probably better. I was told by Mr. John P. Robertson, a merchant of Tilton, Fleming County, who was living about thirty years ago, that Fred Shaw had gambled near that town with a bunch of men one night and about daylight he came in his store to get a bite to eat, and as no one was there but just those two, Mr. Robertson says to Shaw, "Fred is it true that you can throw any point on the dice that you want to?" Shaw never answered, but went on eating his cold breakfast and when he was through, he said to the merchant, "Hand me that blanket there." Pointing to the shelf and taking it he spread it out on the counter and reaching in his pocket he drew out a set of dice, saying to the merchant, "What do you want me to throw?" The merchant called for a point and it was immediately cast before him and after calling for several more, Shaw never missed not even once. Then Shaw said, "Watch this, then I will have to be going." He then cast the dice and a two came up and from there he cast the dice in order to twelve, and started at twelve and went down to the two again, not missing even once. But it had its drawbacks, as Shaw said that he could hardly get people that knew him to gamble.

Shaw, at one time came home, no one knew where from, and he bought a farm near Flemingsburg, paying cash for it. On having it deeded to his parents, he disappeared, no one knew where, or when he would return.

CHAPTER THIRTY-EIGHT

LYNCHING

In order to cover a complete cycle of Fleming County, we have started on the settlement of the County when it was a vast wilderness and those that were helpful — both men and women from the finest heritage of their native state or country — in building this county into a fine prosperous farming community with some of the best productive farms and several nice towns with our share of nice factories. To live the life that we love, to have within a few miles of us the church that we care to worship in, as often as we care to, with no one to disturb us. With all of these nice things, at times there are things that happen that we wish had never happened. I will devote this chapter to some of the crimes that have happened in or near Fleming County, Ky. The stories of these cases are from the newspapers as they were written by various reporters, editors and other records that I have before me. The cases are true, but the names of the ones that were involved are fictitious.

Lynched
Mob Outwits The Officers

*Sy Moses Is Hung By Mob Near Fairview,
In Fleming County*

"This morning, (March 29th, 1920) Sy Moses' body is hanging from a telephone pole on the Maysville and Lexington Pike between Johnson Bridge and Fairview, he having been lynched by a mob of about 40 men last night between 8 and 9 o'clock. The prisoner was taken from a Fleming County deputy sheriff and policemen of Paris last night as he was about to be placed in the jail there. Six autos were standing by the jail, as the officers alighted and started to enter the colored prisoner in the jail. Be-

160

tween the car and jail, the officers thinking that all was well, at once was rushed by a large group of men that was estimated to be as many as forty, with drawn arms, and was told in a quiet and orderly way by their leader, 'We will take this man.' The Sheriff and Paris police at once showed that they meant to protect their prisoner, but in a few seconds the mob of angry men overcame the officers and the prisoner was theirs. Moses was put into an auto and the party made a dash through Millersburg toward Fleming County. A Paris posse was formed and started to follow, but soon gave up the pursuit.

The mob appears to have known every movement of the officers and carried out its plans with utmost precision and clock-like work.

The hanging it is said took about fifteen minutes. Moses made no statement, and the body was not mutilated.

Nine automobiles are said to have been in the procession when it passed through Millersburg. Some accounts say that there were as many as sixty men in the mob. The members of the mob were not masked, but the officers said that they did not recognize any of them. The people of Paris did not realize what had happened until the mob and the prisoner were gone. The mob was in Paris in autos waiting for Moses when he arrived there."

The Crime That Sy Moses Was Accused Of

Last week the tip was quietly given out that Sy Moses, the negro who assulted a young white girl of Fleming County, had been caught in Pontiac, Mich. It appeared that he had boasted of what he had done to a fellow negro in Pontiac with whom he had become intimate. This negro man to whom Moses had boasted, put two and two together and instantly flashed through his mind was the reward money if it were true, and also stating that if it were true, Moses should be brought to justice for the credit of his race. He put himself in communication with the authorities in Fleming County, and finding that it was true and that there was a reward of $500 for his arrest, he went at once to the Chief of Police of Pontiac and arranged for his arrest.

Moses was put under arrest and the authorities here were notified. The authorities here went to Frankfort at once and secured a requisition from Gov. Edwin P. Morrow, and the Fleming County Sheriff sent one of his deputies to Lansing, Mich. and had the requisition honored by the Governor of Mich. He then went to Pontiac where he took charge of the prisoner with whom he arrived in Covington Sunday night.

Monday night the Deputy Sheriff put the prisoner on the train for Paris, Kentucky and on their arrival there, they got off the train and were met by the officers of that city with their prisoner handcuffed. They went by auto to the Paris jail, going by side streets to avoid publicity. What took place from here to Fleming County has already been stated and we can only surmise some of their actions, as they passed through Millersburg at a high rate of speed, some time between 9 and 10 o'clock. That night Moses was hanged to a telephone pole that bore the number 787 on the Lexington Pike, a short distance north of the village of Fairview, or sometimes called Oakwood.

The Fleming County Coroner was called Tuesday morning to hold an inquest and, after summoning a jury, made an inquiry into the facts surrounding the death of Sy Moses. The jury returned a verdict that he came to his death at the hands of the unknown. The hanging seems to have been done in a workmanlike manner, the knot being a regular hangman's noose. The victims hands were wired down to his legs and he still wore the handcuffs which he wore on his trip from Michigan. The body bore no marks of violence. After the inquest was concluded, the undertakers of the local community took charge of the body and conveyed it to their undertaking rooms, subject to the order of his wife.

Fleming County's Judge this morning states that he has not yet been officially notified of the lynching. He states that the law requires an examining trial to be held in the

162

county where the crime was committed, and it was understood that the authorities were to bring Moses to a point near Fairview last night where the Judge was to meet them and, after a hearing, remand him to Covington or some other place for safe keeping.

The Commonwealth's attorney stated this morning that he knew nothing of the plans for safeguarding Moses from a mob and had not been consulted. He says he repeatedly warned officers not to bring Moses any closer than Covington.

The Maysville Independent

The Maysville Independent this morning says the mob was made up of the citizens from about Johnson where the crime occurred and that there were five automobile loads. It says that one member of the mob was left behind at Paris and came down on the train last night getting off at Ewing. He talked freely to the passengers and said that there were fifteen Fleming County men in the party and others from Mason County.

Judge Did His Duty

As showing that the officials of this County did all in their power to protect their prisoner who was taken from the officers at Paris, The Lexington Herald's correspondent at Paris sent to his paper the following: "Paris, March 29th. A well formulated plan to escape the possibility of mob violence went down in defeat tonight when a mob took from the officers of Paris, Sy Moses who had assulted a minor female in Fleming County.

Long before the train arrived in Paris, officials of Fleming, Mason and Bourbon Counties had sought to keep secret the plans to be followed in bringing the negro back to Kentucky."

Flemingsburg, Ky., March 26th

To the Chief of Police, Paris, Kentucky

Dear Chief: A deputy sheriff has gone to Michigan for a negro charged with assault on a young girl. I have directed him to return to Paris with the prisoner and see you. I would like for you to send the Chief of Police in Flemingsburg, the following telegram by Maysville, as it would not be safe to phone here, "The horse was stolen last night at nine oclock or the horse was stolen yesterday morning at six o'clock."

If I receive the one that the horse was stolen last night at nine o'clock I will meet the officers with their prisoner this side of the Lower Blue Licks in Fleming County at nine o'clock at night, but if you say that the horse was stolen at six o'clock yesterday morning, then I will meet you all at six o'clock the next morning. We cannot bring the negro here now and the people think that they are coming back by way of Maysville. Keep this a secret and we will pay you for your trouble. Very sincerely yours, The Judge of Fleming County."

Upholding The Law

In the Paris department of the Lexington Herald of last Friday, we find the following under the above heading: "According to an interpretation of one of the men who helped to take the negro assaulter, Sy Moses from the Fleming County Deputy Sheriff and Paris authorities, when they were about to place Moses in the Bourbon County jail; it was not a mob of law breakers which took Moses from the officers and hanged him in the county in which the crime was committed, but a number of gentlemen organized to enforce the law according to a note tied to the revolver which was taken from the chief of police of Paris and returned to his home in that city. The note was signed John Doe and read as follows:

"My Dear Chief: I have been directed by the person in charge of the gentlemen who took the negro from you Monday night to return to you your gun. I hope that you have not been much inconvenienced by its temporary absence. We regret very much that we were compelled to take the action that we did, but we feel that we kept strictly within the law as the recent legislature passed a law

164

saying that a person committing the crime of rape after being found guilty, should be hung by the neck until dead, in the County in which the crime was committed. We tried the negro and found him guilty, took him to Fleming County where the crime was committed and hung him until he was dead. The crime was avenged, a lesson was taught to others of his kind, and the execution did not cost the State of Kentucky a cent. We wish to express our regrets to the good people of Bourbon County for any undue excitement we may have caused. Respectfully, John Doe. Secretary to the one in charge."

So ends this sad chapter of this affair. It should impress several things on the minds of all, the most important of which is; "Be sure that your sins will find you out, and the way of the transgressor is hard."

Soon after the lynching, the news reporters began to hustle out to get the details of this sensational affair. About 2:30 a.m., the editor was awakened by the reporter representing the Cincinnati Enquirer and The Louisville Courier-Journal, who had followed the party to Fairview, but had left the Lexington Pike and came on to this city, missing the point of interest by a mile or two. He and his party left here about 3:30 and probably they found the place later.

CHAPTER THIRTY-NINE

THE FIRST FIVE HUNDRED
FROM PAPER ADDRESSED TO MRS. NINNIE McCANN

Flemingsburg, Kentucky, Thursday Morning, July 26, 1917

Hiram Duley, Editor-Publisher, Flemingsburg, Kentucky
Issued every Thursday Morning, Subscription, $1.00 a year
in advance

Following are the names and draft numbers of the first five hundred Fleming County boys who will soon be called before the local board for examination for Army service as soon as the official list is received from Washington. This list has been carefully compiled by the local board and the errors, if any, will be corrected when the "Master list" from Washington is received. The quota for this county is 126. Those drafted will appear before the board in consecutive order as noted until 126 are accepted as eligible for service. Thus, the first on the list is 258 Thos. D. Doyle, who will be first for examination, and so on down the line until the quota is made up:

Consecutve No.	Registered No.	Name
1	258	Thos. D. Doyle
2	458	Thos. W. Harris
3	854	Chas. Ashby Peters
4	783	Ernie E. McIntire
5	183	Geo. Crowe
6	1117	Wm. E. Toller
7	837	Jno. R. Porter
8	337	Geo. Lee Garrison
9	676	Green Manning
10	275	Carl Emmons
11	509	Jno. L. Hickson
12	1185	Garcie N. Wycoff

13	564	Harry Saunders
14	945	Alva Thos. Redman
15	596	Chas. H. Jones
16	536	Cray Hull
17	548	Oscar G. Hunt
18	126	Rolla Thos. Conard
19	784	Elmer K. McIntire
20	755	Perry L. McCord
21	107	Robt. L. Crain
22	616	Rolla S. Kendell
23	373	Roger Gibson
24	775	Lee Thos. McIntosh
25	486	Chas. H. Hilterbrand
26	692	Clyde Marion Marshall
27	600	William H. Jones
28	810	Ed. Nelson McRoberts
29	507	Richard S. Hinton
30	309	Addison D. Fleming
31	437	Letcher Hamilton
32	604	Alford Taylor Jackson
33	43	Morton Bell
34	1066	Eber Lytle Story
35	924	William Rolph
36	420	Squire B. Gulley
37	1014	Geo. Riley Smoot
38	1177	James Whittington
39	514	Curtis F. Hopkins
40	433	Cassie H. Hamm
41	11	Herbert Anderson
42	1045	Clell Stone
43	1031	Bert Lee Sparks
44	487	Jas. Hilterbrand
45	797	Wm. Armstrong McKee
46	140	Guy L. Courtney
47	432	Jesse L. Ham
48	18	Clarence Arnold
49	652	John Lykins
50	927	Ray Ross

51	739	Claude Fleming Muse
53	1146	Tilford Estill Vice
52	601	Wm. Roscoe James
54	1103	Walter W. Thomas
55	603	Clarence Burton James
56	606	Arthur Johnson
57	182	Erastus Dean Calvert
58	513	Chas. Hopkins
59	46	Arthur Bellamy
60	1020	Edward Smoot
61	1099	Henry Earl Thomas
62	223	Burt Thomas Davidson
63	117	Geo. Cunningham
64	602	Osel James
65	390	Wm. B. Grannis
66	75	Roy Robert Bradley
67	772	Leslie E. McGregor
68	721	Arthur Morrison
69	788	M. E. McIntire
70	290	Ed Henry Erskin
71	972	Edger M. Saunders
72	983	Albert Saunders
73	757	Clarence McCollough
74	966	Hobert Saunders
75	868	Grover Phelps
76	332	James Fee
77	379	Nealie Grover
78	542	Avery Lee Hunt
79	194	Henry Curtis
80	874	Oliver Perry
81	552	Daniel Charles Hurst
82	298	Blaine Filson
83	675	Eldadoda Manning
84	1143	Geo. T. Vanlandingham
85	343	Chas. Fredick
86	982	Guy Bernice Saunders
87	726	John Moss
88	15	Harvey Earl Argo

89	905	Walter Elmer Porter
90	452	Charles D. Harmon
91	355	Wm. Arthur Foxworthy
92	530	James Cooper Hudson
93	809	Paul Emmit McMannus
94	714	Luther H. Timmons
95	1141	Rudolph Underwood
96	335	Wm. Everett Frazure
97	493	Everett Austin Hester
98	923	Toney Royse
99	341	Geo. Nelson Foxworthy
100	1007	Kirby Taft Smith
101	391	Aubrey Graves
102	353	Jas. Thomas Flora
103	970	Noel Saunders
104	637	Herbert Carl Leet
105	360	Geo. Samuel Gardner
106	1217	John Wm. Zornes
107	571	Omar Dadson Jordon
108	488	Wm. A. Henderson
109	704	Edward Elmer Mitchell
110	72	Elmer Uben Boyd
111	1053	Thos. Allen Story
112	981	Elmer Saunders
113	770	Archie Lane McGinnis
114	882	Ray Peddicord
115	277	Noblett S. Manning
116	749	Clarence E. McCartey
117	1211	William Riley Yazell
118	525	Jon Howard
119	760	John Will McCann
120	645	Harvey Littleton
121	218	Harlett DeRossitt
122	620	Harrison N. Keerans
123	550	Arthur Hurst
124	574	Riley Alvin Johnson
125	31	Addison Bailey
126	56	Harry Clay Bierley

127	792	William Earnest McKee
128	5	William A. Arrasmith
129	350	Harry Flora
130	54	Duard Bevins
131	870	Woodson Power
132	549	Russell Hunt
133	1132	David Addison Turner
134	440	Benj. Cleveland Hamilton
135	1054	Benj. G. Story
136	111	Elmer Mitchell
137	1022	James Marcus Smith
138	841	Calvin E. Pollitt
139	638	Northcutt Lee
140	1032	Millard Springer
141	623	Clarence E. Kidwell
142	269	Riley W. Earlywine
143	685	Chas. Morford Maxey
144	356	Everett Vincent Fleming
145	112	Charlie Crawford
146	1067	Oral Odgen Story
147	128	Jas. Frank Conley
148	697	John Wilson Mers
149	Destroyed in this paper	
150	805	John McKee
151	10	Lee E. Allison
152	900	Addison Planck
153	981	Destroyed in this paper
154	363	J. Parker Garnett
155	1142	Wm. A. Vanlandingham
156	6	Morris Duty Aitkin
157	327	Homer Faris
158	664	Harvey G. Marshall
159	93	John Edward Bryant
160	957	Charles Ramey
161	1112	Benl L. Timberlake
162	345	Jacob D. Faris
163	103	Thomas Eldwood Butler
164	1221	Robert Yantis Thomas

170

165	1102	Walter Gardner Thomas
166	566	Daniel T. Hysong
167	154	Cleveland Colemire
168	51	Elijah Preston Berry
169	717	Estill Mitchell
170	157	Marvin Staggs
171	1073	Wm. Jas. Staggs
172	30	Chas. Lee Bailey
173	199	Clarence N. Carpenter
174	388	Charles Lane Grannis
175	773	Henry Norton McGohen
176	608	Wm. H. Jordon
177	406	Homer Wilson Griffith
178	519	Sherman Hopper
179	25	Noel Arthur
180	392	Clifton Graves
181	889	William Phillips
182	383	Walter Sam'l Gooding
183	1166	Oscar L. Wells
184	588	Allie Pearce Jones
185	856	Russell Pettit
186	705	Silas Edward Mitchell
187	576	Sidney F. Johnson
188	944	Geo. Manse Riley
189	189	Alcis Herman Crain
190	642	James Linvell
191	939	Thomas Rigdon
192	222	Edd Daugherty
193	906	Millard Lewis Queen
194	700	James William Miller
195	1195	James Glover Miller
196	297	William Fuller
197	321	Lon Furgeson
198	736	Sam'l Howe Mulruney
199	628	August Joseph Koerler
200	707	Ambrose Dudley Nineer
201	1002	Oscar Robert Sloop
202	1151	Rolla Vice

203	1101	Oscar Cash Thomas
204	306	Scott Field
205	974	Lewis Elmer Saunders
206	320	Walter S. Fleming
207	950	Clyde Reynolds
208	926	John Ross
209	1010	Tilford Smoot
210	919	Leonard Yantis Royse
211	814	James McRoberts
212	1175	James Whitton
213	1070	Denny L. Story
214	738	Sherman Muse
215	1167	John Andrew Weddle
216	1097	William Thomas
217	1191	William S. Williams
218	848	Harlan Prather
219	1118	Henry T. Tipton
220	121	Clyde Norman Call
221	221	Carol B. Daugherty
222	292	Walter Cyrus Ewing
223	822	John Alton Norton
224	504	William Shouse Hinton
225	1064	Henry Homer Stout
226	1205	Alex Wright
227	1091	Allen Thacker
228	470	Marshall R. Hawkins
229	312	John Martin Fannin
230	90	Thompson S. Brown
231	191	Lester Chafin
232	477	Oscar Bell Helphestine
233	1187	Bruce Otto Williams
234	170	Earl R. Clay
235	753	Clarence McCord
236	130	George Thornton Cowan
237	168	Richard Caywood
238	1023	Forest Snedegar
239	424	Creed Hall
240	840	Arthur Lee Powell

172

241	1188	Ben Williams
242	657	Otho Lytle
243	175	Clyde Crain
244	300	Oscar Fawns
245	278	Owen Emmons
246	1021	Floyd Taten Smoot
247	524	Silas Phillip Howard
248	911	John Rudd
249	1172	John Ware
250	532	Omar H. Hughes
251	1139	Leslie Hollman Turner
252	1214	Wm. Denny Young
253	336	Herman C. Frederick
254	212	Howard H. Carpenter
255	49	John Henry Berry
256	8	Andrew Darnall Allen
257	1160	Ralph Lynam Warren
258	505	William Frank Foor
259	1043	Porter Sam'l Strode
260	1192	Wesley T. Williams
261	557	Joseph A. Hysong
262	662	Arthur Marshall
263	585	John Calvin Jolly
264	1077	Omar Lee Tally
265	781	Wesley McIlvaine
266	1035	Larry Spurlock
267	958	Charles Radcliff
268	323	Clarence S. Faulkner
269	857	Early Prather
270	963	Arthur Saunders
271	438	M. Tabor Hamilton
272	878	Glen Prather
273	1059	John Dye Stewart
274	441	Chas. Wesley Hamilton
275	880	Clarence H. Price
276	357	Clarence M. Gardner
277	23	Grover Hunt Art
278	1173	Samuel Whalin

279	331	James Ellis Faulkner
280	1108	Ben Thompson
281	192	Howard Compton
282	1201	Clarence Williams
283	565	Leonard A. Ishmael
284	1072	Alford Stewart
285	800	Earnest McKee
286	1049	Edward Franklin Staggs
287	715	Harrison M. Miller
288	961	Linnie Sapp
289	539	Claude Humphries
290	349	Charles Yantis Foudray
291	562	Jesse Reed
292	501	Edward Forest Hinton
293	102	Basil Butcher
294	875	Harley Freeman Perkins
295	714	Sherman Mitchell
296	86	Ottie Brown
297	1024	Lewis Snedegar
298	871	Charles Planck
299	1143	Geo. T. Vanlandingham
300	71	William Baltimore Boyd
301	1156	Ora Martin Wagner
302	555	Albert Huston
303	977	Ambrose Sapp
304	506	Frank L. Hinton
305	877	George Phelps
306	435	Alex Hamilton
307	935	Lucien J. Robinson
308	1121	Oppie Lee Todd
309	1150	Omar Vice
310	4?0	Charley H. Harmon
311	113	Ezla Cooper
312	156	Charley Helton Cord
313	725	Owen Aitkin Moxley
314	1004	Ashley Smalley
315	1034	Felix Spence
316	808	Kirby Smith McLean

174

317	789	Stock McKee
318	1183	Taylor Young Williams
319	257	Riley Earlywine
320	567	Shelby D. Ishmael
321	1218	James Medley Zornes
322	421	Uyless Adams Gulley
323	940	Ing Rice
324	169	Walter Cooper
325	436	Millard Hamilton
326	989	Bernard Schwartz
327	1107	Ervin Thompson
328	862	John Calvin Powell
329	257	Pelham Ulyesses Doyle
330	1109	Henry Wash Thompson
331	155	Daniel Pepper Clark
332	284	William Elbert Estill
333	133	James Floyd Craft
334	807	Omar Mastiller McLean
335	867	Harry Frank Purcell
336	930	Earnest Rogers
337	185	Herbie Lee Campbell
338	265	Eugene Davis Dye
339	285	William G. Estill
340	119	Charles Brice Todd
341	1051	Walter Staggs
342	560	William Hysong
343	303	Francis Patrick Fay
344	563	Ira Ernest Insko
345	211	Eckels DeBell Carpenter
346	1163	George W. Warren
347	146	Mace Colgan
348	1049	Howard F. Staggs
349	843	Russell Hedrick Porter
350	1008	Espie Smith
351	229	George Harley Davis
352	410	Bradley Grose
353	299	Ransom Faris
354	1189	Morrell Ogan Winter

355	750	Robert McBee
356	58	Clell Bishop
357	150	James Colgan
358	19	Harvey Tulley Arnold
359	400	Obert Gray
360	4	Lee Brooks Adams
361	115	Harvey Vey Carpenter
362	832	Charley Purcell
363	804	Bruce Owens McKee
364	1180	Oscar P. Wheatley
365	206	Robert Emmit Cullen
366	228	Frank Cleveland Davis
367	136	Louie Cecil Coleman
368	272	Leonard D. Perkins
369	430	James Marshall Ham
370	528	Benjamin David Howe
371	965	Emmit Saunders
372	96	Leslie Burke
373	896	William Plummer
374	1098	Robert Christee Thomas
375	624	Talitha Andrew King
376	507	Richard Showen Hinton
377	665	Edward Dudley Lytle
378	144	John Frank Cord
379	747	Archie Lane McCarty
380	929	John D. Rose
381	901	William Austin Peck
382	1194	Bellville M. Williams
383	138	Olin Hunter Clark
384	91	Edward Brown
385	833	James Taylor Poynter
386	635	William LeForge
387	861	Carl Lee Parsons
388	633	John W. Lawson
389	712	Jerome Mitchell
390	17	Benj. Harrison Arnold
391	802	Emery Cassidy McKee
392	691	Thomas Marshall

393	378	Charles Elmer Glascock
394	1083	Charles Clifton Taylor
395	227	Charles Henry Davis
396	422	Jimmie Guy
397	619	Arthur Grafton Kelley
398	1058	Ollie Thomas Standfield
399	344	Foy Faris
400	824	Cashins Oakley
401	442	Mike Hamilton
402	1213	Curric Morton Yazell
403	202	Leslie Jones
404	164	William Coffee
405	268	Walter Sherman Eckhart
406	272	Simpson L. Emmons
407	1198	Carl Williams
408	1174	Carlin Ross Whaley
409	964	Letcher A. Saunders
410	866	Hugh Hardin Price
411	593	Ervine Jolly Jolly
412	407	Worth Million Grigsby
413	232	Taylor Leander Dawson
414	886	Acie Saunders Perkins
415	883	Elgin Ross Peck
416	1161	Ben Wagoner
417	186	Charles Campie
418	1152	Ollie Ervin Vice
419	776	Clifton McIlvaine
420	566	Tulley Thomas Ishmael
421	582	Ben Franklin Jones
422	541	Grover Cleveland Jones
423	311	Herchell Freeman
424	124	Oren S. Clark
425	481	Carl T. Helphestine
426	895	Chris Joseph Pfeffer
427	744	Elmer Meyers
428	979	George Sauers
429	829	Robert Howe Owens
430	240	Ben Nealis Denton

431	1020	Edmund A. Smoot
432	499	Therman Highland
433	1011	Omar Smith
434	1105	Ollie Frank Thomas
435	444	William Harbett
436	636	Homer Chen'wt LeForge
437	735	Dorsey Mullikin
438	634	Jesse LeForge
439	326	Geardin Faris
440	447	Amos Harmon
441	76	Wm. Thomas Bradley
442	672	Walter Brent Maddox
443	949	Wm. Daniel Reynolds
444	393	John J. Graves
445	993	Rector Carradine Selby
446	1048	Frank Staggs
447	1065	Clarence Aitkin Story
448	861	John Robertson Perkins
449	1181	Henry Otis White
450	158	Henry Hord Crouch
451	778	Porter Lane Turner
452	1	Elza Vaughn Adams
453	187	James Wm. Campie
454	52	Charles Berry
455	105	Frank Campbell
456	660	Thomas B. Lyons
457	838	Matchett Y. Poynter
458	36	James Baty
459	985	Wood H. Saunders
460	352	Ernest Faris
461	418	Morton Gulley
462	920	Frank Royse
463	456	Perry Everett Harmon
464	1176	Earl Whalin
465	416	Henry Clay Culley
466		
467	617	Robert T. Kelley
468	609	Levi Morton Jordon

178

469	613	Chas. Franklin Jackson
470	316	Dr. Arthur C. Fagaly
471	274	Willie Emmons
472	948	Kay Reynolds
473	968	Dave Sapp
474	546	Jack Hunt
475	1154	Landy McDonald Watts
476	766	Alex Theo McFarland
477	754	Clarence S. McCord
478	511	Ernest Honican
479	205	C. Leslie Carpenter
480	913	Lilburne Lee Roe
481	342	Douglas E. Foxworthy
482	860	Samuel A. Parsons
483	934	Richard Robinson
484	427	Herbert Grant Ham
485	666	Cecil L. Maddox
486	241	Chas. Morton Denton
487	40	Leslie Beckett
488	572	Willie Warder Johnson
489	100	John William Bussell
490	1076	Wm. David Swim
491	1138	Curtis Turner
492	158	Willie Grant Craig
493	236	Mathew W. Deering
494	1168	John Weddle
495	214	Harry Evans Cassidy
496	629	James Blaine Lathram
497	647	Ethelbert Hord Logan
498	864	Cecil Harry Pettijohn
499	29	James Edward Bailey
500	918	Omar Dotson Royse

CHAPTER FORTY

GEMS AND FLOWERS

*Every month has its own stone and blossom with
their own meaning.*

January — The garnet and snowdrop, symbolic of constancy, true friendship, fidelity and purity.

February — The amethyst and primrose; sincerity, freedom from care and strife.

March — The bloodstones and violets; strength, wisdom, bravery and love.

April — The diamond and daisy; innocence, purity and peace.

May — The emerald and hawthorne; immortality and a happy domestic life.

June — an agate and honeysuckle; health, wealth, a long and happy life.

July — The ruby and water lily; charity, dignity and faith in love.

August — The sardonyx and poppy; conjugal love and good fortune.

September — Sapphire and morning glory; equanimity and peace of mind, protection against envy and treachery.

October — the opal and hops; hope, purity and courage.

November — The topaz and chrysanthemum; fidelity in friendship and love.

December — Turquoise and holly; prosperity, success, fortune and fame.

180

SOME BIBLE FACTS

The books of the Old Testament, 39.

The books of the New Testament, 27.

Words in the Old Testament, 592,480.

Verses in the Old Testament, 23,241.

Verses in the New Testament, 7,959.

Chapters in the Old Testament, 829.

Chapters in the New Testament, 260.

Letters in the New Testament, 838,820.

Words in the New Testament, 181,253.

Letters in the Old Testament, 2,728,100.

The word "Jehovah" occurs 6,865 times.

The middle book of the Old Testament is Proverbs.

The middle chapter of the Old Testament is Job XXIX.

The shortest verse in the New Testament is John XI:35.

The middle verse of the New Testament is Acts XXII:17.

The longest verse in the Old Testament is Esther VIII:9.

The middle chapter and shortest in the Bible is Psalm XVII.

The middle book of the New Testament is Second Thessalonians.

CHAPTER FORTY-ONE

THINGS TO THINK ABOUT

Mason and Dixon's Line

"Mason and Dixon's Line" is the parallel of latitude 39 degrees, 43 minutes and 263 seconds, which separates Pennsylvania from Maryland, drawn by Charles Mason and Jeremiah Dixon, two distinguished English mathematicians and astronomers. It formed the dividing line between the free and slave states of the original Confederation. This celebrated line properly begins at the northeast corner of Maryland and runs due west. The years from 1681 to 1768 were marked with constant dissenting prorrietaries of Pennsylvania and Maryland and their partisans upon the subject of their common boundary, and the vicinity of this line was the theatre of riot, invasion and bloodshed. The first English Colonies were settled under a grant from King James I in 1606, which gave to two incorporated companies eleven degrees of latitude on the Atlantic reaching from latitude 34 degrees to 45 degrees north, the whole territory having the common name of Virginia. The north Virginia or Plymouth company possessed the north. The south portion of the territory was held by the London Company. Latitude 40 degrees north separated these two Colonies. The north was called New England by Captain John Smith in 1614, while the southern retained exclusively the name of Virginia.

In 1624 the influence of Gondemar, the Spanish Minister, together with his own dislike of popular freedom, induced King James to revoke the charter of both. The unsettled wastes of their territories were now subject anew to the Royal Grant. In 1629 George Calvert, Lord Baltimore, besought the King for a charter of the lands in this region, but died before it was perfected. His son, and successor, obtained from Charles I (June 20th, 1632) a grant which he named Maryland after the Queen, Henrietta Maria.

Know Thyself

March 15th, 1890

The average weight of an adult is 140 pounds, 6 ounces.

The average weight of a skeleton is about 14 pounds.

The number of bones in an adult's body is 240.

The skeleton measures one inch less than the height of the living man.

The average weight of the brain of a man is three and one-half lbs., of a woman 2 lbs. 11 oz.

The brain exceeds twice that of any other animal.

The average height of an Englishman is 5 ft. 9 in.; of a Frenchman 5 ft. 4 in.; and of a Belgian 5 ft. six and three-fourth inches.

The average number of teeth is 32.

A man breathes about 20 times in a minute or 1,200 times in an hour.

A man breathes about 18 pints of air in a minute, or upwards of 7 hogsheads in a day.

A man gives off 4.08 per cent carbonic gas of the air he respires; respires 10,666 cubic feet of carbonic gas in 24 hours; consumes 10,000 feet of oxygen in 24 hours, equal to 125 cubic inches of common air.

A man annually contributes to vegetation 124 lbs. of carbon.

The average of the pulse in infancy is 120 per minute; in manhood 80; at 60 years 60. The pulse of females is more frequent than that of males.

The weight of circulating blood is about 28 lbs.

The heart beats 75 times a minute, sends nearly ten

pounds of blood through the veins and arteries each beat; makes four beats while we breathe once.

540 pounds, or one hogshead—1 one-fourth pints of blood pass through the heart in one hour.

12,000 lbs. or 24 hogshead—4 gallons, or 10,782 and one half pints pass through the heart in two hours.

1000 ounces of blood pass through the kidneys in one hour.

175,000,000 holes or cells are in the lungs; which would cover a surface thirty times greater than the human body.

Bible Errors

Here is a bit of information that I picked from one of my paper clippings. Many editions of the Bible have been published during the last 300 years and into not a few of these some peculiar errors have crept. What is known as the "Breeches Bible" (Genesis, 1560) was so called because Genesis III:7 was translated "They sewed fig leaves together and made themselves breeches," instead of "aprons," as in the English version now used. In the "Treacle Bible" (1568) Jeremiah VIII:22, was made to read, "Is there no treacle in Gilead," etc. instead of "balm" and in 1609 the word was changed to "rosin"; "balm" was first used in 1611. The "vinegar Bend Bible" printed in Oxford in 1717 by John Basket, derives its name from the heading of Luke XX, which was made to read, "The parable of the vinegar." The book had made other errors from which it has also been called after the printers name, "A Basket of Errors." In 1631 a Bible was printed in England and in 1732 another appeared in Germany, both of which made the seventh Commandment read, "Thou shalt commit adultery," the word "not" being omitted. It has since then very appropriately been called the "Wicked Bible."

The Poor Man's Prayer

The rich man has his pew of pride
And velvet stool of prayer;
The poor man's church is very wide,
He kneeleth anywhere.

The rich man says "Thy kingdom come,"
While loathe from this to part;
The poor man prays for "Daily bread,"
Desires it in his heart.

The rich, while with plenty fed,
Still asketh larger store;
The poor man prays for "Daily bread,"
And scarcely meaneth more.

The rich maketh many prayers,
The poor man needs but one;
His broken heart to thee repairs,
And prays — "Thy will be done."

CHAPTER FORTY-TWO

ISSAC VanARSDELL

The subject of this sketch was born in Bath County, Kentucky, April 15th, 1831 and was the son of Issac and Prudence VanArsdell. His father was born in Virginia in 1787, who came to Kentucky with his parents in 1791, landing at the mouth of Limestone (now Maysville, Kentucky), but settled near Harrodsburg, Mercer County, Kentucky. He married Miss Prudence Crouch in Bourbon County, Kentucky in 1816 and settled in Owingsville, Bath County, working at his trade of carpenter and cabinet maker for three or four years. He then moved to the farm he had purchased in Bath County three miles north of Sharpsburg, where the subject of this sketch was reared and attended the common country schools of that day during the winter season at what was known as Poplar Grove, and worked on the farm during the spring and summer season until he was eighteen years of age. He then served a regular apprenticeship of two years at the blacksmith trade with his brother, William VanArsdell. When he was twenty years of age he worked one year at his trade on Cabin Creek in Lewis County, Kentucky. From there he moved to Bethel, Bath County and carried on his trade, doing a large amount of work for two years. Subsequently, he was engaged as a horse and mule trader, driving his stock across the mountains to the Virginia and North Carolina markets, which occupation he continued until the beginning of the Civil War. At the close of the war, he resumed the stock trade profitably until his inclination led him to farming again, when he purchased a farm in Fleming County, Kentucky in 1870, to which he moved.

Mr. VanArsdell was first married to Miss Rebecca Wilson of Mt. Sterling, Montgomery County, on the 19th of September, 1861, who died after four years of their married life, to whom no children survived. On the 25th day of September, 1869, he was married to Miss Laura Lashbrook of Mason County, Kentucky and lived happily together until the 10th day of August, 1896, when she died leaving six children, five of whom were daughters and one son. Mr. VanArsdell was one of the most prominent citizens and farmers in the county, and comands by his exemplary and thoroughly Christian life the esteem and respect of all who knew him. Honest, upright and conscientious in all his dealings with his fellow man. He inspired a confidence in the public mind that but few, if any can surpass — forgiving charitable and just he molded his life by the model of Christian virtue and moral rectitude. If humanity generally were actuated by the kind and generous impulses that control his life and conduct, the criminal code would be a dead letter and good will, harmony and peace would pervade all the avenues of social and public life. Politically, a Democrat, he was placed for years at the head of his party organization, and his acts were always just and his motives pure. He was a faithful and zealous member of the Christian Church. He was ever present to assist in the ministrations of Christian love and fellowship. As an officer and Justice of Peace his judgments were rendered with a sense of impartial justice and his counsel wise and conservative. In private life he was kind and indulgent, exacting only in that which right and duty demands in the exercise of domestic and parental authority, and hence, he elevated his own houshold to the first rank of refined, intelligent social life.

Most of Mr. VanArsdell's descendents have made their home in or near Fleming County, and have followed such professions as teachers and instructors in our public schools, lawyers, farmers and business men of Fleming County.

CHAPTER FORTY THREE

THE HOUSE OF FOUL PLAY

This is supposed to be a true story which took place in Fleming County many years ago and came to light in the year of 1900, when the spirits of the unknown revealed themselves to a ten year old boy in the form of a white sheet or a white calf and talked to him, telling him about dead bodies that were buried under the house where he was living with his Mother, Father and six other children. The house dates back to the early 1800's when it was built of brick that was made on the premises where the house now stands.

About the year of 1867 or 1868 a Mr. A. Sandford, a gentleman of no unlimited means from the state of Georgia, purchased this noted house and one hundred acres of land. At his death in 1899, the farm then went to his daughter, who was then Mrs. Cora Coskery, a widow with a son and daughter, William and Margaret. The Coskery's made this their home mostly in the summer months, going south to their home in Georgia in the winter. Mrs. Coskery died in the 1930's, leaving her two children the farm. Her son, William, who was then married, moved with his family to the farm. The daughter was married later to a southern gentleman by the name of Benittedo. The farm was soon afterwards divided, the daughter taking the buildings and part of the land, the son taking the remaining part of the land and building a new home on it for him and his family. The daughter's family lived most of the time in the South, but later, she lived here alone and died a few years ago in her home here. Soon after her death, her farm was sold to settle her estate — a Mr. Thomas Johnson and his wife bought the farm and, at this writing, July, 1967, are living there with their children.

Now to get back to the records of this unusual story, which I have before me. This story is mostly clippings from

188

old newspapers that have fallen into my hands, which carried the story at the time it happened in 1900.

It was in June, 1900 when a spirit talked to a ten year old boy and revealed to him where twelve human bodies were buried under the floor of the house which was occupied by the boy's parents and children, causing a sensation of suspected murders.

The people of Flemingsburg and the surrounding neighborhood were thrown into quite a state of excitement by discovery of a sensational character, made under circumstances rather mysterious if not supernatural; which in any event goes far to prove the truth of the old adage that "murder will out." The discovery was that of human skeletons found under the floor of the residence of the late A. Sandford. The discovery of this unusual story came to light in June of 1900. As stated, Mr. Sandford bought and moved to this farm soon after the Civil War, and resided there until his death in 1899. Mr. Sandford had no family of his own residing with him for some time previous to his death, his children all being grown and living abroad, and his wife having died several years before this time.

In 1897 or 1898 Mr. Sandford rented his farm to Mr. and Mrs. William Black and their seven children. This family continued to reside upon the premises and occupied the old residence after Mr. Sandford's death.

About the year of 1875, a man who was well-known and well-remembered until 1900, by the name of Bradshaw, by profession a dentist, and therefore, was known as Dr. Bradshaw, took his abode and practiced his profession in the neighboring town of Poplar Plains, about two miles distance from the residence of Mr. Sandford. Dr. Bradshaw, in addition to the practice of his profession, was also the owner of some fine horses, which he had put in training on a track opened by Mr. Sandford upon his farm. For the convenience in the training of his own horses, Dr. Bradshaw left Poplar Plains and took up residence with Mr. Sandford.

After a time, Dr. Bradshaw suddenly disappeared and,

simultaneously with his disappearance, his stock also disappeared. The fact was soon known to the creditors of Dr. Bradshaw. It was thought that he had left for parts unknown to avoid his creditors, but diligent inquiries were made by attorneys in charge of the claims by correspondence to various parts of Illinois, Indiana and other states where it was supposed that he might have gone, but as he nor his property could be found, all further effort was abandoned. The matter of his disappearance soon passed from the public mind, and the name Bradshaw was quite forgotten until the remarkable discoveries of 1900, through a most unusual way. About the middle of that year a sudden revelation was made, which at that time startled the entire community with surprises. Mr. Black's young son, William, then about ten years old, stated that on the previous Sunday afternoon about sundown, while in the barn lot, a white sheet suddenly appeared to him, at which he threw a rock; then the white sheet changed into a white calf. In his fright the boy fled to the house and related to his father what he had seen. His parents endeavored to persuade him that he was laboring under hallucination, and that there was nothing to it. On the following day, near sundown, the boy stated while he was near the barn, the same calf appeared to him. The boy then asked, "What are you doing here?" It answered, "I want to see you." "What is your name?" the boy asked. Upon asking this question the calf disappeared and then a voice said, "I'm Bald Thorn and I want to tell you something about my life." These voices continued to talk with him at various times for some two or three weeks. A few days later when the boy was at the barn late in the evening, again the white calf appeared to him and said, "My name is Bald Thorn, but I was known here as Dr. Bradshaw, the dentist. Many years ago I went to the orchard on the premises to eat some apples. While there I was killed by the discharge of a shotgun." The boy asked what was done with the body. The voice replied "that it was dragged by two men, one at each arm to the trap door in the corner of a room in the house and was buried in the corner from the trap

190

door, under the floor in the same room about twelve inches deep."

Upon these statements of the boy to his parents, a few days later they proceeded an investigation as to their truth. Beneath the trap door was a small excavation of not more than three or four feet square, the floor being at all other points a distance varying from one to two and one-half feet from the ground. The floor was raised at the point designated by the boy by Joseph Secrest, Mr. Smithers, Mr. Kissick, and Mat Deering, neighbors of Mr. Black and upon moving the dirt to the depth of twelve or fifteen inches, human skeletons were found and other bones that looked like human bones such as ribs, also the end of the humorous, two or three meta carpal and clavical bones, and other small bones that appeared to be those of an infant. Fragments of clothing were also found with the bones.

Mr. Black and his son, with Mat Deering, came to Flemingsburg and brought the bones to the office of Dr. H. C. Kehoe, who compared them with the bones of the human body. The boy was unwilling to separate himself from these relics, as he was admonished by his ghostly visitor to take charge of the remains and inter them in the Locust Grove near by, then it would cease all further communication with him. Upon this information, he was permitted to return home in charge of the relics.

The boy claimed to be in almost constant communication with this and other of his mysterious companions, whose voices he claimed that he could call upon and talk to at will. He claimed that the remains of six men, three women and three children were buried under this house. Mr. Black and his wife became nervous and frightened and moved from the premises, the scene of such mysterious visitations. The voice, through their son, assured them that all that was wanted from them was the removal of the remains and a decent burial. The parents of the boy were plain and simple people, the boy was sprightly and talked with a degree of intelligence far beyond his years. When communicating with voices that he claimed to hear, he looked ahead with a peculiar gaze, with his eyes fixed straight ahead and other features rigid. Upon the whole, there was mystery behind all of this that was never solved. The first was the mystery of the revelation, and the second was the un-earthing of some foul deed, if the revelation was true. The writer has no record of what became of the bodies, although there are a few people still living in that community who remembers this story well.

CHAPTER FORTY-FOUR

GEOGRAPHIC FACTS

The citizens of Fleming County are most all American born, but of mixed ancestry and therefore are mixed by intermarriages. Some of them can hardly trace their lineage, but these crosses are the basis of making many and useful citizens and able men and women, who are bringing their county to the front ranks, classing her with the best in the State.

According to the record that I have, Fleming County has given six Governors to other states and, at the same time, has always filled her own offices with good and capable men.

Fleming County has furnished to other states and territories men of ability who have occupied high places as Legislators; to Ohio, Indiana and Missouri Governors, with three Governors of U. S. Territories; she gave to Cincinnati, Ohio a Mayor and to western Territories a delegate in Congress and two high Judicial officials; to the Southern Confederacy she gave a Brigadier General and three Congressmen; to Virginia, a Legislator and a high Sheriff to Richmond, Virginia on the James. Fleming County has also furnished two State Grand Masters to the Masonic Order and one to the Independent Order of Oddfellows. She has given to other counties and states, lawyers, preachers, teachers, doctors, husbands and wives — the trend is ever increasing with no sign of ever weakening.

In Fleming County there is an odd formation of earth that has drawn attention far and wide, even to other states, and countries as far away as South Africa. This unusual piece of earth is located on what is now state Highway No. 32, about six miles east of town. There is approximately six acres of ground that nothing has ever grown on except where leaves and other matter have lodged long enough to decay. There maybe will be a tuft of wild grass or a small bush that might extend to a height of only a few inches (and this is very rare). There are no rocks, gravel or soil of any kind on this odd piece of ground. It is called Blue Bank, as it is extremely blue and waxy. In the center of this six acres there is a deep formation of about one thousand feet wide in the shape of a giant bowl. Inside of this depression, in places, there are several piles of the same blue substance with a waxy content, that reaches a height of fifteen to twenty feet. The road now going through part of this odd piece of earth has destroyed part of its natural curiosity, but the site still gives one an odd feeling, to say the least. The bowl-shaped depression gives one the thought of some Godly power deep under the ground with unlimited force which in time had forced its way to the surface.

Some years before the turn of the 19th century, a stranger (a soldier of fortune), who had worked in the diamond mines of South Africa, traveled through this part of the country, came across this strange formation and, after a careful examination of the strange blue substance, he pronounced it very much like the diamond fields in Africa. But of the thousands of people that have visited Blue Bank in the last hundred and fifty years with the hope that they be the first one to find a sparkler, no one has had success. This strange piece of Fleming County was owned for years by the Fants of the County. After the death of the last survivor of the Fants, this piece of property was sold and the Campbell Brothers, Cliff and Clyde, bought the Blue Bank and are the owner of it at this time.

Traveling about six miles east on the same road from Blue Bank, one will enter into the mountain region. Here a good many years ago, geologists examined the specimens of a mountain and pronounced it rich in iron ore, but because of its location and the low price of iron, there is little hope that any mining will be done. Enough iron ore has been dug from the sides of this mountain to justify its name, as it is known as Iron Mountain.

On the Flemingsburg and Elizaville Pike one mile west of Flemingsburg in the year of 1803, the brick house of

Mr. Robert Andrews was built on a track of land that was owned by Mr. Andrews. This farm was later owned by his sons, Robert and Seth Andrews. The farm is now (1967) a nice sub-division of Flemingsburg. Also the same year, the two-story brick building on West Water Street in Flemingsburg was built next to the then Exchange Bank, which for a number of years was the site of the famous Bon Ton Cafe owned and operated by Mr. T. H. McDonald. The building now houses another business.

In the year of 1865, there was an oil well drilled in Flemingsburg, at a depth of approximately one thousand feet. They struck no oil, but was compelled to quit on account of gas.

In 1869, in the northwestern section of Fleming County, the Kentucky Central (now L. & N.) R. R. built the first railroad in Fleming County. The next railroad was the Covington, Flemingsburg and Pound Gap.

The dirt was broken on this road on October 24th, 1876, by Mrs. Robert Samuels who then was living in Poplar Plains, Kentucky. The first regular run of this road was in the spring of 1877. This railroad changed hands several times, as well as names, and in 1908, was called The Cincinnati, Flemingsburg and Southeastern Railroad. There has been only one railroad wreck that has amounted to anything in Fleming County and it has been described before in a chapter by itself.

The biggest loss by fire in Flemingsburg was September 1st, 1905, when seven business houses and all, or most, of the merchandise in them was completely destroyed, with many other buildings partly destroyed.

In 1890 the Flemingsburg Graded High School Building was built. This building has been replaced with a larger and better building in another part of town. School was discontinued in the old building several years ago, the building being condemned, and has been sold to Mr. and Mrs. William Sims, Mr. and Mrs. Marvin Suit, and Mr. and Mrs. Jerry Rosser. They all are prominent business people of Flemingsburg.

One inch of snow fell on Fleming County and this section of Kentucky on the 20th of May, 1894. It has never been equaled or passed since. I have heard those say, that were living at the time, that roses were in bloom and how pretty they looked partly covered with snow. The snow was so heavy that it was the cause of several trees breaking down and limbs breaking off of many others.

The greatest drought that Fleming County has ever known was in the year of 1854 and Wm. Cord that year had to haul water from Garr Pond, a deep hole in Fleming Creek at the site of Martha Mills, a distance of six miles to Flemingsburg, to run his flour mill. That has been stated as the mill that Mr. Fant owned and operated.

The record of the first store that was ever opened in Fleming County, was at Flemingsburg, and was opened and run by Thomas Wallace in the year of 1804. The first hotel was opened by Mr. John Faris in Flemingsburg in the same year, 1804.

In the year of 1816 there was a church known as the Old Cedar Church and it was torn down in the year of 1882. The location of this church has never been found by this writer.

In the year of 1908, there was another great drought, but it did not surpass the drought of 1854. It is on record that it did not rain from the month of July until Christmas.

CHAPTER FORTY-FIVE

AN OLD ACCOUNT BOOK OF 1792

Mr. E. H. Kenner, a Flemingsburg business man, while exploring the garret of the old Court House of that city on May 3rd, 1897, found an old account book, which was quite a curiosity and had attached to it an interesting history of the town and county. Other books and papers were also found by Mr. Kenner which he gave to a local newspaper of the County in the month of May, 1897. The following is copied from that newspaper article:

"The book was evidently kept by some of the Stocktons and the first charge in it is dated Mt. Pleasant, Ky., May 20th, 1792. Some think that the name Mt. Pleasant was formerly applied to Flemingsburg, but not one of our oldest citizens can recollect of our city ever being called by that name. The general opinion among our oldest residents is that Mt. Pleasant was the old homestead name of the Stockton Place, which was situated near the stockade which enclosed what is now known as the old Stockton Spring, located about one-half mile west of the city.

"Among the charges in the book are many names that were familiar here years ago, but no where is it stated by whom the book was kept. Evidently, it must have been kept by some of the Stocktons, as George Stockton, and other members of this pioneer family, are in many instances charged with cash and other items.

"The book is an ordinary leather back book, yellow with age, the paper being unruled but of a good quality. It seems to have been in use several different times and by different persons. In the first part of the book the accounts of a general merchandise business were kept running from 1792 to about 1800. While further over are a number of blacksmithing accounts. In the back part, also, are to be found the personal accounts of George Stockton, where he has each one of his children charged with cash, land, and other articles. There is also to be found in the book several agreements or contracts properly drawn up and signed.

"The first item in the book is a charge to Patrick Allison for two and one-half gallons of whiskey, for one pound and two shillings, dated May, 1792. Pat must have been pretty fond of his toddy, as he is frequently charged with liquor! After that, at another place, he is charged with one buck skin, nine shillings, six pounds of tobacco, four shillings and six pence. Four flints are marked against Pat also at another time, when no doubt he was preparing to go on a rampage against the Indians. The four flints just cost him four pence. In the first part of the book, i.e. from 1792 to 1804, the charges are all entered in English denominations —pounds, shillings and pence. After 1804, dollars and cents are used.

"It is quite interesting to look at the old book and imagine oneself carried back to 1792 in Fleming County, and also to note the articles sold and compare prices with those of today. Fleming County at that time was a wilderness, inhabited partly by Indians and abounding with all kinds of wild game. An Indian is now a curosity and the bears, buffalo, deer, wild turkey and many other game that was so plentiful have long ago left the land. What another century will bring forth would be hard to predict.

"A record of town lots is to be found in the back part of the book, which shows the price of lots in Flemingsburg, some containing as much as four or five acres at that day ranged from five to twenty-five pounds each.

"Below are a few of the charges taken from the old book: Daniel Peck, one pound tobacco, four shillings, six pence; three-fourths yards calico, five shillings, three pence; one yard muslin, three shillings; one pocket handk'f, four shillings, six pence. To Henry Smith, four and one half pounds pewter, six shilling, nine pence. George Stockton, cash, eighteen shillings. Thomas Sweet, one set of knives and forks, nine shillings. George Stockton, three pounds of coffee, nine shillings; one pair cotton hose, seven shillings, six pence. William Secrest, one dozen needles, seven shil-

198

lings, six pence. William Kennan, sharpening plow, nine shillings.

"Major George Stockton and his half brother, Col. John Fleming, were the original settlers of Fleming County, having located here in the year of 1787. The names of both are found frequently in the book, and the County took its name from the latter, although he (Col. John Fleming) did not settle in Fleming County at first, as he went to Strodes Station in Clark County, only remaining there for a year or so, and then he returned to Fleming County and there established the Fleming Fort. In the closing years of the eighteenth century, there were just three settlements in what is now Fleming County — Stockton's, Fleming's and Cassidy's.

"On Feb. Second, 1789, Robert Stockton was killed by hostile Indians on the banks of Fox Creek and his grave is still to be found where he died. His companion named Rhodes was also wounded at the time and dragged himself fourteen miles, when he was picked up seven days later on the banks of Fleming Creek which was too high and prevented his crossing.

"William Kennan, whose name is frequently mentioned in the old book, was a conspicious figure in frontier life and was noted for his swiftness on foot. More than once he saved his scalp from the Indians' tom-a-hawk by his fleetness at running, and his adventures and narrow escapes would fill a volume. He was the great-grandfather of Mrs. Larry Howe, who lived in this County and was well known. William Kennan died in 1827.

"Michael Cassidy, a forefather of the Cassidy's who resided in this City and County, is another whose name appears a number of times in this book. Mike was small in statue, but nonetheless venturous in spirit. He passed through a large number of thrilling experiences with the Redskins and always came out best. He died in 1829.

"Another amusing feature of the old book are several accounts of trips to Cincinnati. On the first in the list of itemized expenses is one quart of whiskey. On the next

trip three quarts were required, and on the third, five quarts
are entered. Each trip it seems required a little more liquor,
some of which was purchased at Washington, Mason
County, as the trip was made over land."

CHAPTER FORTY-SIX

MY OLD KENTUCKY HOME

From an old newspaper dated 1899 is a story of how the song of My Old Kentucky Home was written:

"Federal Hill is situated only a mile east of Bardstown, Kentucky. It was here that one of the most touching and famous songs of the century was composed and sung. This old Kentucky home had been in possession of the Rowan family for nearly a century. Judge Rowan, once a United States Senator from Kentucky, and during his day one of the most famous jurist in that section, resided there for years. His son, the Hon. John Rowan, Jr. who was a man of splendid intellect and who held high official position during his life time, also lived there until his death. After his death his widow, once a lady of great beauty and renowed popularity and who even in her old age retained much of these spendid gifts, had resided. It was here that "My Old Kentucky Home" was composed and sung.

"One beautiful morning while the darkies were at work in the corn fields, and the sun shone with mighty splendor upon the waving grain, first giving it a color of light red, then changing it to a golden hue, there was seated upon an old bench in front of this historic mansion two young people — a brother and sister. High up in a treetop a mocking bird warbled its sweetest notes. Over in the hidden recesses of a small bush the thrush's mellow song could be heard. A number of small darkies were playing near the not faraway door. The air was refreshing, just one of those May mornings when all nature seems so beautiful and the feeling of everyone so comfortable. The young man was of medium size, with a strong and pleasant face. Beside him was seated a young woman of great beauty. Her hair hung over her shoulders in long tresses; her form was symmetrical and her face was unusually beautiful. When the brother and sister had finished the first verse, the fair girl took the paper from his hand and sang in a soft, sweet voice: 'The sun shines bright in my old Kentucky Home! 'tis summer, the darkies are gay; the corn top's ripe and the meadow's in the bloom, while the birds are making music all the day. The young folks roll on the little cabin floor, all merry, all happy, all bright; by 'n by hard times come a-knocking at the door— then, my old Kentucky Home, good night.'

"On finishing the first verse the mocking bird descended to a low bough. The feathery songster drew his head to one side and appeared to be completely enraptured at the wonderful voice of the young singers. When the last sweet note had died away upon the air her fond brother, who had just finished the chorus, sang in a deep bass voice: 'Weep no more my lady O, weep no more today, we'll sing you a song for the old Kentucky Home; for our old Kentucky Home far away.'

"The darkies had laid down the hoe and the rake; the little tots had placed themselves behind the large, sheltering trees, while the old black women were peeping around the corner of the mansion. The faithful old hound dog, that lay basking in the sun, never took his eyes off the young singers. Everything was still, not even the stirring of the leaves seemed to break the wonderful silence. Again the brother and sister took hold of the remaining notes and both sung in sweet accents another verse; 'They hunt no more for the possum and the coon, on the meadow, the hill, and the shore — they sing no more by the glimmer of the moon on the bench by the old cabin door. The days go by like a shadow o're the heart, with sorrow where all was delight; the time has come when the darkies have to part, then my old Kentucky Home, good night.'

"The thrush and the mocking bird drew closer and closer to the singers as they continued; 'The head must bow and back will have to bend, Wherever the darkies may go, A few more days and the trouble all will end, in the fields where the sugar cane grows. A few more days to tote the weary load — no matter, it will never be light — a few more days till we totter on the road; then my old Kentucky Home, good night.'

"As the singers finished, tears flowed down the old darkies cheeks. The very little children emerged from their hiding places with broad smiles upon their faces. The mocking bird and the thrush took wings to their homes, while the old hound dog still lay basking in the sun at the feet of the beautiful young maiden. The young man was Stephen Collins Foster and his sister, Eliza C. Foster. Both were residents of Pennsylvania, but upon this occasion had come to Kentucky, upon the pressing invitation of Judge Rowan, to pay him an extended visit. Stephen Collins Foster was the composer of many beautiful songs, but none of them equalled "My Old Kentucky Home."

CHAPTER FORTY-SEVEN

PROGRAMME

CONCERT

M. E. CHURCH, SOUTH
Flemingsburg, Kentucky

THURSDAY EVE., DEC. 19, 1878

Part First

1. Anthem _____ Full Chorus

2. Dancing O'er The Waves _____Quartette
   Misses Slicer and Kenner, Messers. Cooper and Young

3. Last Rose of Summer _____ Inst. solo
   Miss Elle P. Cane

4. Baby Mine _____ Duet
   Mrs. Mary Andrews and Daughter

5. Down Among The Lilies _____ Trio
   Misses Cane, McConnell

6. John Anderson, My Jo _____ Duet
   Mrs. T. L. Given and Mr. Charles Dudley

7. Come Where The Violets Blow _____ Duet
   Mrs. Andrews and Miss McConnell

8. Rock of Ages _____ Tableau
   Miss Fannie Armstrong

9. Selections From Il Trovator _____ Inst. Solo
   Miss Addie Stockwell

10. Grandfather's Clock _____ Solo and Quartette
    Miss Given, Miss Kenner, Messers. Cooper and Given

11. The Song of Home _____ Solo
    Miss Ella P. Cane

12. The Farmers and His Girls _____ Sextett
Mrs. Given, Mrs. Andrews, Misses Throop,
Kenner and McConnell, Mr. Cooper

Second Part

1. The Chasse _____ Duet — Piano and Organ
Misses Cane and McConnell

2. Union March _____ Inst. Solo
Miss Arthusha Stone

3. Starry Waves _____ Solo
Miss Thersia Slicer

4. La Chass Infernale _____ Duet
Misses Cane and McConnell

5. You Know _____ Duet
Miss Slicer and Mr. Steers

6. By-Gone Days _____ Solo
Mr. James S. Cooper

7. Select Reading _____ "Dora" _____ Tennyson

8. The Ten Virgins _____ Misses Slicer, Cane, Stockwell,
Dudley, Singleton, Mullay,
Armstrong, Troop, Kenner and
McConnell

9. Good Night _____ Full Chorus

CHAPTER FORTY-EIGHT

SOME KNOWN FACTS OF FLEMING COUNTY, KENTUCKY

This chapter will be condensed from things about Fleming County that are known by this writer and from the records of Fleming County that I have, also from a small phamplet of Fleming County that was written by Mr. Dan T. Fischer of Flemingsburg in 1908.

My records tell me there were no Indian tribes who made Kentucky their permanent home when the white man first invaded the western wilderness that was and is known as Kentucky. All the tribes had an agreement that Kentucky would be kept as a private hunting ground for them and to exclude all others, friend or foe, but hostile tribes frequently invaded their hunting grounds, and for that cause great battles were fought between them. This being true, probably, was the reason this part of Kentucky had many Indian burying grounds that could be found in about any section of this part of the State until several years after the twentieth century, and some are still visible, also several Indian mounds (now preserved) can still be seen.

To add strength to this belief, in the earlier part of the twentieth century a good many of these mounds were opened. The contents were always the bones of an adult warrior probably slain in these conflicts, and buried with some, would be found a tom-a-hawk, an arrow, a flint or some other small trinket that was loved by the Indian.

In the year of 1796, the town of Flemingsburg was laid out and two churches were erected in 1799; the Methodist Church was built by Stockton's Station and the Presbyterian Church was built where the Flemingsburg Cemetery is now.

One of the most famous battles (and probably the most famous) that was ever fought between the whites and Indians in Kentucky was fought at the Battle of Blue Licks in what is now Fleming County, on August 19th, 1782, with the whites losing sixty-five men.

The first child born at Stockton's Station was a boy in 1788, and his name was Lake Stockton.

Fleming County was hit by the dreaded disease of cholera, two different times; in 1833 and again in 1855, and as the saying goes "Truth is stranger than fiction"; in the year of 1833 the total deaths by cholera was 65 and the most deaths in one day was 9. In 1855 the total deaths was 65 and the most deaths in one day was 9; the deaths being the same in both years.

Fleming County had its first legal hanging in September, 1828, when Dan McLoughlin was hung.

The first Fleming County Court House was built in 1829.

The first turnpike in Fleming County was built in 1836 and was between Flemingsburg and Maysville.

A two-story stone house was built two and one half miles from Flemingsburg on the Mount Sterling turnpike in 1800 (now State Highway 11) by Thomas Benton. This famous old house was later owned by Mrs. Sue Hendrix Lytle Peck, now owned by her son, Mr. Hendrix Lytle. (This old land mark was destroyed by fire a few years ago and has been replaced by a modern new home). It is now occupied by Mr. Harry Horn who operates the farm there.

Thomas Wallace, a wealthy slave owner, who did not want to hold his slaves in bondage any longer ordered them set free, and at his own expense, sent them back to their native country, Liberia. Mr. Wallace had educated a slave whom he had given the name of Val Todd, who after being in his native country a few years, became its Governor. These slaves were freed and sent to their native country in the year of 1842.

A Letter From Poplar Plains, Kentucky
By A Twelve Year Old Boy
Who Signs His Name Only As Incognito

October 1873

Dear Editor: Sir: Having noticed in your paper that you wished news from different places in the County, although I am only twelve years old I will send you something from our town, Poplar Plains.

The town of Poplar Plains came into existence and began forming a town sometime between 1790 and 1800. It took its name from a large poplar grove that stood where the town now stands. Our town contains two drug stores, two dry goods, two groceries, a Post Office, a number one Hotel, two churches (Christian and Methodist), two blacksmith shops, one cooper shop, one buggy shop, about fifty houses and two schools. Our town has not improved much in the last few years, but from the spirit of the times, I think progression is visible. I imagine some of our citizens are contemplating of having a Fair ground, and race track, for horses are on the brain here both young and old. On Saturday last, we had a colt show, premium offered by Theodore Hart, Esq. for the best and second best of "Rukewoods" Colts; John Scott of Tilton and Andrew Hedrick of this place judged. The first premium was awarded to Rawleigh Kendall and second to Willie Samuels. "King Tom," a bald chief colt, the property of Theodore Hart has made better time than three minutes. He is now in the hands of Jno. Neil of Maysville. There are several fine animals here among them "Alamo," the property of Theodore Hart, Rawleigh Kendall, R. F. Dearing; "Rukewood," a race horse belonging to Theodore Hart, and "Almont," the property of R. F. Dearing.

Our town is occasionally aroused from its dullness by its railroad men. Col. R. J. Samuels, the Vice President of the C. F. & P. G., and the President, Jno. T. Sullivan, were in town last Friday as was Mr. Seymore with his corps of engineers. They have been surveying a route from West Liberty to Pound Gap. They have finished and are now surveying the route up from Covington.

Our town has been unexpectedly called upon to mourn the loss of one of our most estimable ladies. Mrs. Elizabeth Samuels, aged 72 years and 4 days, is no more. How suddenly death bites. She leaves a great many friends to grieve after her. She lived the life of a Christian — she died the death as such. Tell me how a person lived, I will tell you how they die. Funeral discourse by Elder G. S. Kinberly, and the remains interred in the Flemingsburg Cemetery.

Signed Incognito. Well written by a twelve year old boy.

FLEMINGSBURG COLLEGE

J. and M. P. Eckman, associate Principals, will open a school in Flemingsburg College which is now undergoing thorough repairs, on Monday, September 1st, 1873; at the following rates of tuition:

Greek, Latin, German and French Languages,
    per session of twenty weeks _____ $20.00
Common School Course _____ 15.00
Primary Department _____ _____ 10.00
Piano Taught Daily _____ 20.00

A reasonable charge to each music scholar to cover expense of keeping up the instrument kept in the College building. Pupils charged their proportion for fuel. No deduction for absent days except by special arrangement with the teachers.

CHAPTER FORTY-NINE

THE SLAVE BOY

There are several versions of this unusual colored boy who grew up in Fleming County, Kentucky. As I, the writer, can well remember this person, I will use the story that was told most often by him, also I will state here most of the dates related by him or by people who knew him better than I. The story begins as thus:

Some time in the 1840's, a baby boy was sold in the New Orleans Slave Market in the arms of his mother. It was supposed that they were bought by the owner of a ship, as the mother who was an unusually good cook, applied her skill as the overseer of the ship's kitchen.

These dates or the name of the ship are not known, but it is assumed that they made more than one trip up and down the Mississippi and Ohio Rivers from New Orleans on the Mississippi to distant cities, such as Memphis, Tenn., Cincinnati, Ohio, Maysville, Ky., Huntington, West Virginia as well as Pittsburgh, Pa., and probably many other towns and stops.

However, this slave mother and her young son got to Fleming County, sometime before the 1850's in the hands of a family by the name of Arnold, who was living at that time in the eastern or southeastern part of Fleming County, near the town of Hillsboro, Ky.

This colored boy grew into a free man in Fleming County and was known as Uncle Joe Simons. His mother died while she made her home with the Arnold's. The boy soon after the death of his mother, left that part of Fleming County, Ky. He took up residence near Tilton, also in Fleming County, with a family by the name of Walkers, and later, with the Fitch family, who were related and well known families of Fleming County, and have descendants living in the County at this tme.

Uncle Joe, as the boy was later known, grew to be

one of the most quoted, most remarkable and most mysterous men of the entire County of Fleming.

As Uncle Joe grew from a child into early manhood, he had one paramount burning desire — the desire to learn to read. Slaves, however, were forbidden by their owners to acquire any such skill, as education was believed to put radical ideas into otherwise docile minds.

There were two different stories told over the County about how Uncle Joe learned to read. One was that his Mistress was a student of the Bible, which she read aloud several hours every day, with the Bible laid open on her lap. The then small boy stood at her feet with a long stick with a large piece of paper fastened to it which was cut in narrow strips and was waved over her by the boy in a slow motion so as to keep the flies off her; so in this way it was said by many people that the boy became an apt student of the Bible, although he could not read any thing but the Bible, and it had to be in an upside down position.

Another story of this unusual boy-man's ability to read and understand so much about the Bible, came to light in 1930 when it was supposed that Mr. Thomas Bowden, a prominent Fleming Countian who had been living in Madison, Wis. (and I believe that he was a prominent newspaper man) had told many people about Uncle Joe Simons and many stories of him. This story had drawn the attention of world-famous Robert L. Ripley, author of Believe-It-Or-Not, so in 1930, Mr. Ripley, or one of his staff members, interviewed Uncle Joe and he wrote about him in his articles of Believe-It-Or-Not. Uncle Joe also told many of his friends this story about his ability to be able to read.

The power of providence proved to be strong in favor of Uncle Joe. He stated to them, that many tortured nights of praying to be given the ability to read, Uncle Joe one night heard a voice telling him to turn his Bible upside down. When this was done the passage before his eyes became meaningful to him, and ever after this, he could read the Bible if it was kept in an upside down position. So delighted was the young man with this ability to read, that he read, and reread his Bible until he was so adept in its formation that any passage could be quoted, and he could give its location, as well as quote the verses preceding and following the one dictated. He later learned to write his name, but this also was always upside down and backwards. Uncle Joe was one of Fleming County's famous characters.

It is sad to close this chapter on Uncle Joe, who died on the County Poor Farm, after many years of being able to read nothing except an inverted Bible. Uncle Joe died in the late 1930's and I will close this chapter by copying his death notice in the Fleming County Paper.

"Aged Colored Man Called by Death. Joseph Simons, aged about 95 years old, one of Fleming County's most widely known colored citizens, passed away Monday at the County Farm at Crain Creek after a short illness. One of the County's most colorful characters, he was noted for his ability to quote any verse in the Bible by memory, the Bible being the only book that he could read and he could only read it up-side-down and backwards. A few years ago this feat gained him a place in Ripley's Believe-It-Or-Not.

"He was said to have been born the son of slave parents, but had spent many years in Fleming County. He had resided at the County farm for the past several years. Rites were conducted at the County Farm with Rev. Cooper in charge and burial was made there."

CHAPTER FIFTY

GROUND HOG DAY

Last Sunday, Feb. the second, was Ground Hog day here in Fleming County. As I was turning through my books, I found his picture with a story about this age-old and mythical weather prophet. The story is headed thus:

Groundhog makes debut today;
But hunts a hole if sky ain't gray
Six more weeks of winter feared
If beast sees shadow of his beard;
He must have whiskers, cause he's as old as sin,
Says rhymester who brought this ditty in
Since naughteen hundred and gosh knows when,
Since the time when man was two-thirds chin,
Since the day when Adam was led astray,
We've believed in the Legend of Groundhog Day.
The groundhog's a wary, suspicious beast,
Of all his worries, the weather's the least.
On February Second, no matter where,
He halts his nap and comes up for air.
He strolls out in the broad daylight
And looks at the sky and takes a sight.
He looks at the East, the West and sech
And takes a chew and takes a stretch.
If the day is cloudy he expectorates,
Wipes mouth with hand and then he prates,
"Musta been a long winter an' I figure how
I'll stay out, 'cause it won't be long now."
If the day's all bright, he shakes his head
And drops his chew and goes back to bed.
He says, "It wouldn't be right I fear,
To be sunburnt this early in the year."
If he stays out, winter soon will end,
But if he goes back in his den,
The storm will rage and wind will roar
And we will have bad weather for six weeks more.

213

CHAPTER FIFTY-ONE

ATLAS OF FLEMING COUNTY, KENTUCKY

By D. J. Lake & Company 1884

Sherburne Precinct No. One.

The main towns in Precinct No. One were Sherburne and Concord.

The Sherburne business references of that year are listed as thus:

J. R. Scott, manufacturer of fancy brands of flour, which we have on hands at all times for sale, also saws and all kinds of lumber to order.

Browning & Trumbo, dealer in dry goods, groceries, notions, hats, caps, boots, shoes, crockery, glass and Queensware, tin and hardware fine ready-made clothing, and all goods usually kept in a first-class country store. Also highest prices paid for country produce.

Mt. Carmel Precinct No. Two .

The main towns in Precinct No. Two were Mt. Carmel, Foxport, and Mt. Gilead.

The Mt. Carmel business references then were:

Cook and Adams, dealer in dry goods, drugs, groceries, hats, caps, boots, shoes, ready-made clothing, hardware, tin, china and Queensware.

T. A. Henderson dry goods, groceries, hats, caps, boots, shoes, paints, oils, putty, glass, coal, oil, pure spices — druggist, patent medicines, notions, etc.

Mrs. Morrissey & Son, Proprietors of the Morrissey House, also dealers in dry goods, groceries and everything usually kept in a first-class general store.

C. E. Proctor, Physician and Surgeon.

A. M. Wallingford, Physician and Surgeon.

J. R. Luman, Miller and Distiller.

W. M. Collins, Dealer in leaf tobacco.

J. M. Wallingford, Farmer and Justice of the Peace.

M. P. Wallingford, Farmer and Justice of the Peace.

Foxport business reference:

Million & Cumber, Dealers in dry goods and groceries, also leaf tobacco.

Poplar Plains, Precinct No. Three.

The main towns in Precinct No. Three were Poplar Plains, Wallingford, Hamburg, Sanford (now Goddard).

Poplar Springs Precinct No. Three business references were:

J. D. Muse & Co., Dealers in dry-goods, groceries, hats, caps, boots, shoes, hardware, Queensware, tinware, clothing, notions, fine toilet soap, tobacco and cigars, and all goods, usually kept in a first-class country store and residence at Hamburg, Fleming County, Kentucky.

E. H. Jones, Contractor and Builder. All work entrusted to me will be done in first class order.

A. H. Colburn, teacher and artist, Wallingford, Fleming County, Kentucky.

Poplar Plains business references:

B. A. Plummer, dealer in dry goods, notions, clothing, hats, caps, shoes, boots, hardware, Queensware, tinware, glass and crockery-ware, cigars, tobacco, etc.

J. H. Samuel, Physician and Surgeon.

R. D. Weaver, Physician and Surgeon.

Mrs. Mary E. Hord, Proprietress of Hotel, keeps a first-class hotel where the traveling public can be accommodated at any and all times.

Hillsboro, Precinct No. Four.

The main towns in Precinct No. Four were Hillsboro, Grange City, Ringos Mills, Farmville, Sunset, Stringtown and Spring Hill.

Hillsboro business references:

C. H. Davis, agent for German Insurance Co. of Freeport, Ill. and Pheonix of Hartford, Ct.

R. M. Zimmerman, dealer in Italian and American marble and all kinds of marble work, Corner of Main and Church St.

C. R. Garr, Physician and Surgeon.

John Clark, Hotel and Livery Stable Proprietor.

J. W. Crain, Dealer in groceries, hardware, drugs, medicines, boots, shoes, notions, etc. A full line of goods usually found in a general store.

E. M. Money, dealer in dry goods, clothing, boots, shoes, hats, caps, hardware, Queensware, cutlery, paints, oils, patent medicines, cigars, tobacco, stone, tin, and woodware, in fact everything generally found in a country store, and will be sold as low as the lowest. All kinds of produce taken in exchange for goods at highest market price. Groceries a specialty.

Store at Sunset, two and one quarter miles southwest of Hillsboro, Ky.

R. Tulley Arnold, dealer in dry goods, groceries, hardware, notions, Queensware, glassware, hats, caps, shoes, etc. Goods exchanged for produce at market price.

Store at Farmville.

Grange City business references.

W. R. Howard, dealer in leaf tobacco and grain.

C. W. Roberson, blacksmith and wagon maker. Repairs of all kinds promptly attended to. Horseshoeing a specialty.

F. W. Gray, carpenter and builder. All work promptly attended to. Also work in the undertaking line will receive care and attention.

Howard Walton & Co., dealers in dry goods, notions, groceries, hardware, Queensware, glassware, boots, shoes, hats, caps, drugs, and medicines. A full line of goods at lowest possible prices. Produce taken in exchange for goods at liberal prices.

Tilton Precinct No. Five.

The main towns in the Tilton Precinct were: Tilton, Bald Hill, and Balm (generally called Concord).

The Tilton business references were:

J. B. Sousley & Co., dealers in dry goods, groceries, hats, caps, boots, shoes, hardware, Queensware, harness and saddlery, tinware, notions, clothing, fine toilet soaps, cigars, tobacco, and all goods usually kept in a first-class country store. Country produce taken in exchange for goods.

216

W. B. Scott dealer in dry goods, groceries, hardware, Queensware, tinware, hats, caps, boots, shoes, notions, clothing, cigars, tobacco, and all goods usually kept in a first-class country store.

Store and residence, Martha Mills, Fleming Co., Ky.

Wm. Grannis, Practical Surveyor.

Robert McKee, Stone Mason and farmer.

Marshall McCann, Manufacturer of fancy brands of flour. For sale, brands and ship stuffs and dealer in posts, rails and lumber.

W. F. Hendrix, contractor, builder and farmer.

Centerville, Precinct No. Six.

The main towns in Precinct No. Six were: Ewing, Cowan, Centerville, Fairview (also sometimes called Oakwoods), Evans Mill (now known as Evans Corner).

Centerville Precinct business reference were:

J. H. Blair, farmer and dealer in coal.

A. H. Ishmael, dealer in leaf tobacco.

Coleman and Buchanan, dealer in dry goods, groceries, hats, caps, boots, shoes, notions, cigars, tobacco and all goods usually kept in a first-class country store. Fairview.

G. L. Carter dealer in dry goods, groceries, hats, caps, shoes, boots, notions, hardware, Queensware, tinware, clothing, cigars, tobacco, etc. Also dealer in leaf tobacco, Fairview.

John M. Moore, Justice of the Peace and farmer.

W. S. McCord, Justice of the Peace and farmer.

J. R. Crawford, dealer in leaf tobacco and farmer.

C. W. Hammond, dealer in leaf tobacco and farmer.

W. W. Weaver, blacksmith and wagon-making done in first-class style. Horseshoeing a specialty.

Jas. S. Swart, dealer in leaf tobacco and farmer.

T. H. Caywood, teacher and farmer.

L. G. Cord, teacher and farmer.

Theo. Alexander, Postmaster, Adams exp. agent and agent for K. C. R. R. at Cowan.

Alexander and Williams & Co., dealers in dry goods, groceries, hats, caps, shoes, boots, notions, fine ready-made clothing, crockery, glass and Queensware, tin, hardware, and all goods usually kept in a first-class country store.

Store and residence at Cowan, Ky.

Flemingsburg, Precinct No. Seven.

Flemingsburg, being the County seat and the largest town in the County, had no other town or village near it.

The Flemingsburg business reference in 1884 were as follows:

County Officers

C. H. Ashton, Clerk Circuit Court

W. F. Howe, Sheriff

R. B. Kendall, Deputy Sheriff

J. McHowe, Deputy Sheriff

A. F. Vize, Deputy Sheriff

Jas. W. Shouse, Mayor and Attorney

R. K. Hart, Representative

M. M. Teager, County Attorney and Master Commissioner

Harvey H. Kendall, Marshal

Lawyers

Wm. Hendrick, Attorney-At-Law

M. M. Teager, Attorney-at-Law

John P. McCartney, Attorney-At-Law

Jas. W. Shouse, Attorney-At-Law

Wm. H. Cord, Attorney-At-Law

W. A. Sudduth, Attorney-At-Law

Physicians

L. McDowell, Physician and Surgeon

P. A. Gordon, Physician and Surgeon

Dr. Waugh, Dental Surgeon; office at residence, two miles north of town

Banks

David Willson's Exchange Bank

Fleming County National Bank

Publishers

Hiram Duley, Editor and Publisher of Times Democrat

C. D. McCartney, Editor and Publisher of Fleming County Gazette

218

Merchants

W. A. Roby & Co. in hardware, stoves, groceries, boots and shoes.

VanSant & Bro., dealers in staple and fancy groceries, dry goods, clothing, boots, shoes, etc.

A. T. McDonald, dry goods, notions, clothing, boots, shoes, hats, caps, Ladies and gents furnishing goods, furniture, etc.

Jno. T. J. Reynolds, dealer in pure drugs, chemicals, paints, oils, varnishes, dye stuffs, fine stationery, toilet articles, perfumery, etc. Physicians' prescriptions carefully compounded at all hours.

Miscellaneous

R. S. Hudson, Auctioneer and stockbroker.

Wm. S. Fant, Proprietor Flemingsburg Mills.

T. M. Fleming, Proprietor livery and sales stable.

Geo. Faulkner, Superintendent of Flemingsburg Cemetery. Florist and dealer in marble.

G. L. Palmer, agent for the Continental Home, Phoenix, Royal, Niagara, Lancashire, Louisville Underwriters, New York Underwriters, Firemen's Fund, Star, American Central and Travelers Insurance Companies.

L. F. Bright Proprietor City Hotel.

Wm. H. Harrison, Carriage maker, repairing promptly attended to.

Jas. M. Sousley, Agent of Kentucky Grangers Mutual Benefit Association of Georgetown, Ky.

Muses Precinct No. Eight.

The main towns in Precinct No. Eight were Muses and Fox Spring. The Muses Precinct business reference were listed as:

E. Muse, dealer in dry goods, groceries, clothes, cassimeres, hosiery, gloves, cravats, teas, coffee, sugar, molasses, rice, fruit, salt, spices, fish, soap, candles, starch—saleratus, soda, cordage, wrapping paper, twine, cutlery, glass, putty, paints, oils, garden seed, wallpaper, notions, farming implements, etc. Produce taken in exchange for goods.

Elizaville Precinct No. Nine.

The main towns in Precinct No. Nine were: Elizaville, Nepton, Johnson Junction and Sapp.

The business reference of Precinct No. Nine were:

L. B. Abney, Physician and Surgeon, also dealer in pure drugs, medicines, chemicals, paints, oils, dye stuffs, varnishes, stationery, toilet articles and a full line of hardware.

J. N. Proctor, Physician and Surgeon.

Henry M. Scudder, Minister, Presbyterian Church.

F. M. McIntyre, Stock trader.

D. D. Allen, dealer in all kinds of agricultural implements and mill machinery.

Captain John M. Gray, Turnpike Contractor.

W. H. Stewart, dealer in dry goods, groceries and all kinds of general merchandise.

R. H. Dodson, teacher.

Eli Planck, dealer in staple and fancy groceries and farm produce.

Wm. Bell, dental Surgeon.

Sapp business references:

Jarvis T. Rolph, dealer in general merchandise. Country produce taken in exchange for goods.

Kirk and McDonald, dealers in leaf tobacco.

Wm. Geary, Justice of the Peace.

Plummer's Mills Precinct No. Ten.

The main towns in Precinct No. Ten were: Plummer's Mills, Plumber's Landing, Franklin Mill, Bell Grove Springs.

Plummer's Mills business reference:

Campbell and Yeazell, Proprietors of corn and flour mill, custom work solicited.

Plummer's Landing business reference:

O. L. Hinton, dealer in dry goods, groceries, provisions, hardware, Queensware, ox yokes, ox shoes, raw hides of all kinds, fur pelts in season, etc.

J. R. Evans, dealer in general merchandise, country produce taken in exchange for goods.

J. W. Gilmore, clerk and book-keeper for O. L. Hinton.

220

T. W. Cooper, carpenter and proprietor of the Plummer's Landing Hotel.

James Hollan, Proprietor of Plummer's Landing Mills.

Franklin Mills business reference:

W. H. Hinton, farmer and miller.

Dr. J. P. Huff, Physician and Surgeon.

CHAPTER FIFTY-TWO

FLEMINGSBURG AND FLEMING COUNTY'S WORST STORM ON RECORD

Flemingsburg, Kentucky, Sunday, May 28th, 1925

On Sunday morning about eight o'clock, May the 28th, 1925, a heavy black cloud arose in the west and northwest. This cloud being so dark and angry looking that it at once drew the attention of all the people far and wide. As deep rolling thunder added to its threating appearance, disaster seemed to be getting closer and closer. At a little after nine o'clock the storm broke over the little modest town of Flemingsburg. The wind sung a shrill accompaniment through the telephone wires and followed by a torrential fall of rain that had never been seen before. There was no hail in the town of Flemingsburg of any consequence, and the only damage there was the blowing down and up-rooting of numerous shade and fruit trees. One of the most handsome sugar maple trees, which had a circumference of nine feet and ten inches, and which stood just west of the F. & N. R. R. Depot, was snapped off as if it were only a straw.

Only a short distance from the city of Flemingsburg, there was the heaviest hail storm that was ever experienced in Fleming County. The worst hail seemed to have fallen in the vicinity of Tilton, Bald Hill and the Smith neighborhood on Allison Creek. At the home of Raliegh Lee (The Old Wilson Home) near Tilton there was plenty of hail on the north side of the buildings until the next day, while at the home of James E. Smith, near Allison Creek, they gathered up hail in sufficient quantities to freeze ice cream for their Sunday dinner. With it all, it seemed that the hand of Providence was there, too, as there were no lives lost and not a dwelling house was completely wrecked, though the dwelling on the Peter Carpenter farm (now owned by Mr. Gilbert Havens) just below Martha Mills (then occupied by Mr. William Perkins and family), was partly un-roofed and slightly damaged.

222

The Perkins family escaped injury by fleeing to the cellar that was nearby. The home of Leslie B. Newman (now owned by his daughter, Mrs. Noble McKee), in the same vicinity, lost a new veranda that was blown away by the wind. All of the windows in the home of Sam F. Fleming were broken or blown out by the hail or wind, and heavy damage was done by the water at the home of Mr. Fleming which stood near Allison Creek.

Other buildings blown down or damaged by this storm were barns and other farm buildings. The Bald Hill orchards of Mr. V. C. Razor and the Amyx-Tolliver folks were not seriously damaged by the hail, although several trees were uprooted. Mr. Matt Smith, whose home is on Allison Creek, had a field of nice alfalfa hay just about ready to cut. It was almost beaten into the earth by the hail and many tobacco plant beds were destroyed as well as garden stuff.

Chickens and turkeys were a great factor in the farmer's life in raising his family. The chickens supplied the family with eggs, meat and some cash money the year around, while the turkeys, as a rule, were owned by the farmer's wife; if they were early and fat they were sold for the Thanksgiving market, but if they were late they would be kept for the Christmas market. The wife would sometimes receive as much as two hundred dollars or more. With this amount of money, which in those days seemed a large amount, the housewife would buy warm winter clothes for the entire family and most always had some left over to buy something new for the home, or keep for a rainy day. The chickens and turkeys that were in the path of the hail and rain storm in Fleming County were scarce in the year of 1925, as many were killed or drowned and some women suffered severe injury on account of being caught out in the storm while trying to save their flocks.

It was related that a girl on the farm of John O'Connor on Allison Creek was out trying to save the chickens and the wind became so strong that it was about to carry her away. She grasped a small tree and it was torn up by the wind and snatched from her grasp, leaving her prostrate on her face, and she was nearly beaten to death by the hailstones.

Livestock exposed to the heavy hailstones also suffered greatly, but there was no known deaths, although some stock was found in other fields with no known way of getting over good fences except by the force of the wind. A large draft mare with a young mule colt on the farm of Mr. Theodore Hart of Tilton was seen to hover her colt under her. The colt was saved from harm, but the mare was covered with bumps and bruises from which she recovered in a few weeks.

I have been able to get the names of most of the people who lost barns or other buildings, but probably not the entire list. They are as follows: Coming from the north, the first seems to have been on the farm of Mrs. James McFadden near Helena; R. W. Darnall, two barns, one insured and one uninsured; R. H. Sousley Heirs, two barns; Charles Thompson, barn; Hart Bros., two barns; D. M. Brown, barn; W. W. Rogers, barn and windows blown out; Lowman Barbee, barn; Sterling Tally, barn; Mark Hendrix, barn; Dow Carpenter, barn; Mrs. Mary Mitchell, barn; Clete Johnson, barn; Bruce Saunders, barn; James S. Rawlings, barn; Avery Saunders, barn; Mrs. James McGinnis, barn; Theodore Hart, barn; Mrs. Noble Peck, barn; Mrs. Lizzie Simonson, barn, no insurance; John O'Connor, barn; Fred Hinton, barn; Frank Davis, barn; Allen Lytle, barn and among others who suffered minor damages were C. W. and J. P. Robertson, W. F. Sims, James E. Smith, Bruce McIntyre, Newt Hurst, W. M. Jackson, Luther Timmons, Albert Nealis, also Mr. J. B. Booton of Tilton suffered a total loss of his private orchard of several trees.

Most of the losses mentioned were covered by insurance in the Fleming County Mutual. I am not able to give the total loss sustained from this storm but it was heavy. At Mt. Carmel, no buildings were blown down, but the streets were blocked for several hours by shade trees that were blown down and limbs broken off of others.

Dr. Clyde L. Garr of Flemingsburg was caught in his

Ford Coupe on the Poplar Plains pike, near the residence of Mr. Harvey Magowan (now the home of Mr. and Mrs. Albertice Foudray). He had quite an experience. The glass windows in his new car was broken out, also the top, hood and fenders, as well as the rest of the body of the car showed a severe beating by the hail stones.

A large tree was blown down on the farm of Mrs. James McCreary, falling across the electric transmission line, breaking connections with Maysville, the current being shut off for several hours, but being Sunday very slight inconvenience was caused by it. Other losses that ranged from $1,450.00 down were:

Thomas Calvert	$ 5.00
Heber Campbell	7.50
Mrs. D. D. Sousley	32.20
A. J. Doyle	8.00
Eliza Harmon	2.25
Wren Watson	35.00
Jas. F. Hutton	35.00
Bruce Saunders	3.50
Albert Nealis	500.00
A. E. Saunders	203.00
Jas. H. Sousley, ad.	1,450.00
Jas. H. Sousley, unadjusted	
Mrs. Sue Peck	700.00
C. W. Robertson	7.50
John Ferguson	2.00
Orie Cornette, unadjusted	
Marshall Arnold, unadjusted	
George LeForge	6.50
W. T. Crain	7.25
Mrs. Dora Selby	5.00
Mrs. Moran	12.85
A. L. Denton	2.50
M. C. Colliver	2.50
Thomas Gray	8.00
W. F. Sims	25.00

J. J. Walton, Est., unadjusted ___ __ _____

John O'Connor _____ 400.00

John O'Connor, unadjusted _____

Another point of interest that might be given on the day of this storm, concerns Mr. and Mrs. Jack Denton and their two daughters, Virginia, who is now Mrs. Harlan Kissick and Helen, who is now Mrs. Earnest Hamm. Mr. and Mrs. Denton were waiting patiently for the third arrival of their family, and at the very hour that the storm was raging at its highest, they were presented with the third member of their family, a son named J. W. Denton. He is now married to the former Miss Bonnie Emmons and they have two children, a boy and a girl. The Dentons being large land owners in Fleming and Bourbon Counties, so J. W. and his family are living on one of their farms on Allison Creek near his birth place, where he is engaged in raising grain, livestock and tobacco.

CHAPTER FIFTY-THREE

THE LOST TOWN OF GATH IN
FLEMING COUNTY, KENTUCKY

The author of this book came to the town of Tilton in Fleming County, Kentucky in the year of 1935, that being the same year that he married Miss Virginia Ellis Hart, the daughter and only child of the late Theodore K. and Mary Marshall McCann Hart, who resided in Tilton, Fleming County, Kentucky. Tilton lays five and one half miles south of Flemingsburg, the County seat of Fleming County, Ky. Nearby was Locust Creek and Licking River and the small town of Locust. The waters of the two streams named above were noted far and wide for the abundance of fish of several different kinds. At that time, living between Tilton and those two nice streams of water, was a man by the name of Mr. Russell G. Harmon, who owned over a thousand acres of good farming land which joined the waters of Locust Creek and Licking River at several places. Mr. Harmon at that time was an aged man and a retired farmer of Fleming County. He had lived in that part of Fleming County all of his life. He was also very fond of fishing, so he and I would take tents and all the supplies that we would need and go to the best fishing places and camp and fish for a week or more at a time. Our fishing would be with trot-lines and also by the old fashion way with the cane poles. Our luck for the most of the time was good. We would always set our tent on the banks of Licking River, which was owned by Mr. Harmon. As soon as our tent was erected, all of our supplies were in, our trot-lines baited and a few hand poles set, Mr. Harmon would hunt a large flat rock, dig a pit, and so arrange the rock over the pit to make us a stove on which to do our cooking. In this way we enjoyed ourselves for days at a time, cooking our fish and other food that we would have on hands. We most always used minnows with which to bait our lines, so at noon each day we would take our seine and minnow buckets and go to the Locust Creek for our supply of bait for the next day. On these trips to the mouth of Locust, at the Licking River there were hundreds of acres of good fertile land with very little or no elevation at all, and it was noticable at that time by the shape of the ground and some foundation rocks, that once there had been buildings there. Back from the banks of the Creek and River, several hundred feet, the ground elevates to the beautiful hills that form one of the most beautiful spots in Fleming County. This site is now included in the hundreds of acres of farm land owned by Mr. John Graham, who lives with his family in a nice modern brick home which he built.

Through my inquiry from Mr. Harmon and others, I was told there was once a town laid off there by the name of Gath. All that I could find out then was from the older people of the community, and they would tell stories about the town of Gath that their parents or grandparents had told them years before. So my effort to find out the story of Gath never stopped and about a year ago I was talking with Mr. Jason Payne, who lives a few miles east and upstream from where the town of Gath was formed. Mr. Payne has long been a friend of mine and is one of Fleming County's best historians. He had been interested in the town of Gath and has many records about it, which he had obtained through research of many hours of work and records. So through some of his records, which he has been so kind to let me have for this story, I am indebted to Mr. Jason Payne of Hillsboro, Kentucky.

The following is the information which I have obtained from various records. The town of Gath materialized for a brief time only, then sank into oblivion. This information about Gath comes by research of the First Court records, dating back to the year of 1798. These records are well preserved. In the year of 1798, upon the motion of Byrom Routt, a court order was secured setting aside 140 acres of land at the Mouth of Locust, in Fleming County, Kentucky for a town that was to be named Gath. (Gath is a Biblical name dating back to Noah's ark). Apparently travel was

228

from Flemingsburg by way of Cassidy Creek to Fleming Creek where there was LeForge's Mill, (now known as Martha Mills or Martha's Mill).

In the following year, it was ordered that two buildings be erected for the storage and inspection of hemp and flour. That leads us to believe that the people then were raising hemp and wheat in the fertile bottom lands of the Locust-Licking community. The hemp would be made into ropes and clothing and the wheat would be ground into flour that was to be floated down the Licking River by a small craft or probably a raft.

In a court order of May, 1799, it was decreed that John Hunt and Manley Brown go to, and inspect, at the Mouth of Locust on the Licking River in the town of Gath, and mark out by meters and bounds as much land as they thought sufficient, but not exceeding two lots of one-half acre each, at the most convenient and proper place where to erect warehouses and funnels, and make a report to the Fleming County Court. In the deed book at page 338 is the platted map of Gath. There were 115 lots in all. One lot consisting of two and one half acres, the streets were 32 feet wide with a 8 foot alley at the back.

The February, 1801 Court order book has this information. Upon the motion of William Burke, it was decided to establish a ferry across the Licking River in the town of Gath at the end of Main Street being opposite the road leading from Mt. Sterling, Ky. The Court not being advised, continued the matter to the next court with leave for the parties to introduce any legal testimony.

A January, 1802 court order gave a ferry grant to cross Main Licking River at the town of Gath and agreeable to law, order that the rates be as follows: wagon and team, four shillings; man and horse, nine pence; a person on foot, four and one half pence; sheep, hogs, and horned cattle, one pence each; every carriage of two wheels, two shillings.

The November court records of 1800 show that William P. Ramey came into court and gave bond and security agreeable to the law for operating a ferry across the Main Licking

River at the town of Gath in Fleming County.

It is stated that in the year of 1796 Byrom Routt owned one-third interest in 6,212 acres on both sides of the River and in 1795, William Burke owned more than 1300 acres.

At the same time they were looking for a road to the Mouth of Flat Creek (now Sherburne) with that road being built probably caused the flow of traffic to by-pass Gath and go through Sherburne, as the town of Sherburne developed for a number of years and the town of Gath never developed, and except for old court records has passed into the unknown.

This all happened just a few years after the battle with the Indians on the Battle Run Creek in Fleming County. Stockton's Station (now Flemingsburg) was the only town in Fleming County at that time.

In the year of 1800, the census of Flemingsburg, Ky. was given as 124 population. Remember in the days when the town of Gath was laid out the travel was by ox cart and horseback with saddle bags, and sometimes a pack horse. Most usually the ladies were on side saddles and the mothers with their babies in their laps.

At that time Fleming County had no County seat, so could it have been in the mind of those sturdy pioneers who tried so hard to build the town of Gath on the banks of Locust Creek and Licking River, with thousands of acres of good building land for a town or a city, and many more thousands of acres for good farms to make this town the County seat of Fleming County? If so, and if they had started a few years later, maybe they would not have failed.

CHAPTER FIFTY-FOUR

THE MARRYING SQUIRE OF GRETNA GREEN OF THE OHIO VALLEY

The small town of Aberdeen, Ohio, located on the banks of the Ohio River opposite Maysville, Kentucky was noted as a matrimonial center for a number of years. It was called the "Gretna Green of the Ohio Valley," so named for a small Scotch border town. In the early 1820's, Thomas Shelton was Justice of the Peace and lived in a log cabin at Third and Locust Streets. In this capacity and during his 95 years of living, he married many thousands of couples who were eloping from Ohio, Kentucky, Indiana, Illinois, Missouri and most of the Southern States.

At the close of the Civil War and following Thomas Shelton's death many widows and orphans of soldiers had trouble getting pensions because these marriages performed by Squire Shelton were questioned as to whether or not they were legal. Later, they were declared legal by an act of the Legislature.

Following Thomas Shelton as Justice of the Peace was Massie Beasley, who made Aberdeen even more popular than his predecessor, as he was thought to have married more than 20,000 couples.

Thomas Green Beasley, the Squire's son, was pilot of the ferry boat, The Gretna Green, which crossed the Ohio River between Maysville, Kentucky and Aberdeen, Ohio for a number of years. Many marriages were performed on board this boat as Squire Beasley went daily to the wharf looking for couples to marry. He never would marry a couple without license until he reached the Ohio shore, but while crossing, he would question the bridegroom and determine from this interview what his fee would be. He would accept nothing but cash with few exceptions. One of these exceptions was from a couple from a neighboring town who paid the fee in potatoes which they brought down in baskets.

After the death of this wife, her husband was married by the Squire for the second marriage. This time he paid the Squire $20.00.

Not all of the couples who were married by Squire Beasley were eloping. They came from New Orleans arriving at the Squire's house by carriage, sleigh, horseback, or in a skiff. Some were barefoot, dressed in sunbonnets, others arrived handsomely attired in silks and satins. A true story which was told to the writer by his wife's grandmother is as follows: When the approaching wedding of Ninnie Faris to George McCann, my wife's grandparents, was known by Ninnie's first double cousin, Thomas Faris, Tom asked her where she and George planned to be married. Her reply was "The parlor of the Hotel in Maysville." Her reason for not wanting a home wedding where her two older sisters had been married by their grandfather, James Moran, a Methodist Minister, was the fact one sister in making her vows had said "I do" twice for which they were still teasing her, and Ninnie did not want any one of her family to hear her wedding vows. Tom Faris and Myma Lee wanted to be married in a double ceremony with Ninnie Faris and George McCann. Myma Lee's father was dead, her mother was living in Lawrence, Kansas, and since Myma was under age, she would need her mother's consent to be married in Kentucky. She and Tom had planned to go to Aberdeen to be married by Squire Beasley, persuading Ninnie and George to go with them. The two couples stopped at the Hotel in Maysville and made reservations for their rooms for that night, August 12, 1891. Due to the high water, the ferry boat was unable to make the crossing, so the two young men and the two young ladies, who were dressed in taffeta and lace were rowed across the rain swollen river in a skiff. Ninnie, knowing the disposition of her cousin, Tom, had warned him if he made any wisecracks she and George would come back to Maysville and be married as they had planned, since they were both 21. Tom displayed his best manners until they reached the Ohio shore. As they walked up the wharf, as usual there were several people waiting to see who was in

232

the wedding party, then Tom said in a whisper, "Want to go to a wedding?" Ninnie heard the whisper and gave Tom a look that he always remembered, but a few of the people followed for the ceremony. Their witnesses were A. L. Hudson and Mae Waldron. Squire Beasley gave each couple a post card picture of himself and The Gretna Green which is highly treasured today by my family.

According to the story of *The Gretna Green by Dorothy Richardson that appeared in the Louisville Courier-Journal on August 4, 1897, and again in The Valley Times on November 14 and 21, 1968 — "It was the wedding parties which came by horse back that were especially welcomed by the small boys of the village, who were able to earn many an honest penny by holding the pawing thoroughbreds for a few moments before the Squire's door, while the ceremony was going on inside. Sometimes, however, and, in fact very often, there was no time to dismount, as there was danger in delay when an irate father, brother or guardian, armed with a brace of pistols followed close behind. Many a night or early morning has the Squire been rudely awakened from his dreams by the firing of a shot under his chamber window, which signal he well knew. The smoke would not be cleared away from the discharged weapon in the bridegroom's hand before the drowsy Squire would emerge from his doorway and perform the ceremony right then and there, the bridal couple remaining on their horses.

"One incident which the people of Aberdeen delight to relate in recounting the many merry adventures of the Squire of Aberdeen, is the elopement of a prominent Kentucky couple, the bridegroom being later a United States Congressman from one of the Western States. This was an elopement in every sense of the word, one of the blood-and-thunder kind. The girl's father and brother were in hot pursuit of the runaways and were heavily armed. There had been

---

*The Gretna Green by Dorothy Richardson which appeared in The Louisville Courier-Journal, August 4, 1897. Reprinted in The Valley Times, November 14 and 21, 1968.

a feud between the families of the contracting parties for generations, and the father of the bride vowed that he would kill the lover rather than permit him to marry his daughter. The pursuers were so near that the noise of their horses hoofs could be heard distinctly when the Squire poked his head out of his chamber window in answer to a volley of shots. The Kentucky Lochiary flourishing a pistol in each hand, swore roughly at the delay, and when he espied the Squire's night-capped head he roared for him to come down and marry him at his own price, but to come quickly or he would be a dead man. Squire Beasley was then in his seventy-eighth year and was too stiff in the joints to dress himself quickly, so he appeared before the excited couple wrapped in a log-cabin bed quilt and shod only in his socks. Standing under the branches of a gigantic sycamore tree, and arrayed like a patriarch of old, the Squire mumbled over a hasty marriage ritual at the conclusion of which the new-made husband flung him a well-stuffed wallet and dashed away toward the hills with his hard-won bride. The fugitives disappeared in a cloud of dust just as their pursuers came dashing up the street to find that they had been foiled and that the Squire had stolen a march on them.

"The thrilling circumstances of this elopement were not uncommon or unusual in Squire Beasley's time, as representatives of many a feudal faction have fled to him and found consummation. It is the only case on record, however, where he sacrificed his personal appearance for the sake of any wedding, however important. He was what is known as a dressy old man; in his youth he had been something of a Beau Brummel, and even in his old age he betrayed much vanity as to the cut of his hair, the fit of his coat and the tying of his cravat. That this vanity was inordinate is evident from the large number of photographs he had taken of himself. It is probable that there is not an actor on the stage today who has posed for his picture oftener than did Squire Massie Beasley. He ordered them not by the dozen, but by the gross, and that he must have used a great many gross during his official career is certain from the fact that he always presented the bride with a photo when he handed her the marriage certificate.

"As was mentioned before, the Squire's son, Thomas, was pilot of The Gretna Green and as he is said to have received a commission on every bridal couple whom he landed on the Ohio shore, it goes without saying that he was not idle during all these years. When an agitated and breathless couple came hurrying down to the ferry boat, with an infuriated father or guardian following close at their heels, it was Thomas Beasley who calmed their fears by the assurance that he would see them safely over and that he would not give their followers an opportunity of boarding the boat. And he was always true to his promise. As soon as the elopers had crossed the gang-plank, the pilot ascended to his station at the wheel and the good Gretna Green was turned toward the green shores of Aberdeen. Nor were any threats or prayers on the part of the gesticulating parties in pursuit strong enough to deter him from his purpose of landing his passengers on the borders of the land of promise. Seeing they were thus foiled, the enraged and outwitted parents were wont to follow in skiffs, then there was excitement not only for the boat's crew and the contracting parties, but also for the residents on both sides of the river. The pilot had his own code of signals which he had arranged for the purpose of faciliatating his father's business methods. Everybody knew when The Gretna Green emitted six, short, sharp shrieks of her whistle that there was a chase to Aberdeen, and it was then a race between Squire and the people to see who would get to the landing first. Long before the boat had touched shore, every man, woman, and child in the town, who was able to run, walk or crawl had congregated about the Squire who was taking the situation through the immense "spy-glass," which he always carried for that purpose. He was always ready for such emergencies, his vest pocket containing a goodly stock of blank marriage certificates and, as his marriage ceremony was short, he made quick work of an elopement once he stood face to face, or even within earshot of the refugees.

"One unlucky day the Gretna Green was disabled, and into that afternoon an excited couple arrived at the wharf in proverbial "wedding haste" but could find no means of transit. It was during a period of high water and the skiffs which lie about the landing were all in use. At last with much pleading and the promise of $10.00 as a reward for his services, the owner of a small boat agreed to row them to the opposite bank. Before they had reached the middle of the stream the girl's father appeared on the scene, and Lord Ullenlike offered $20 to any man who would row him across the river. When they had almost reached their haven, the bridegroom committed the fatal mistake of looking backward and, unable to surpress his exultation at seeing his pursuers baffled and outwitted, he jumped to his feet and enthusiastically waved his hat in the air, which demonstrative action caused him to lose his balance and pitch headlong into the current. While some of the spectators on the shore were rescuing the unfortunate man, the birde's father overtook and carried her off, tearful and frightened, while the thwarted bridegroom was left lamenting. The most desperate elopments transpired under cover of darkness. The night watchman of the Gretna Green made more money than the boat itself by hiring out skiffs to the runaways who came down to the waters edge at all hours of the night in quest of some means of transit to Aberdeen.

"The people of this city and vicinity were married by Squire Beasley as a matter of course, as were also his own townspeople. Three scores of fathers and mothers of families in this region whose grandparents were married by Squire Shelton during the early part of his regime, whose parents were married by him in later years, and who were themselves married by Squire Beasley, illegality of marriage running thus through three generations. Saturday and Sunday night were favorite times for the people here to be married, especially, those employed in the cotton factory and about the wharf.

"While considering this open and long-continued violation of the law, as carried on by the two Squires of Aberdeen,

236

the question naturally arises in the readers mind as to why these men were never prosecuted, and why the people of the town stood by and suffered their laws to be thus ignored. The apparently perplexing query is readily explained by the old adage, 'A kind heart covers a multitude of sins.' A more popular man than either of these rollicking careless old Squires never trod the earth, and if they made money easily and in a questionable way, they in turn spent it just as freely among their neighbors and fellow townsmen. Especially, was this true of Massie Beasley. While shrewd and exacting in his business relations with the matrimonially inclined, no begger ever went away empty-handed from his door, nor did a neighbor or friend in financial extremity ever have aught to say in denial of the Squire's generosity. But rather than tempt the enforcement of the law, Squire Beasley preferred that his worldly gain should be represented by a bank account rather than in real estate. Immediately upon his election to office, he very wisely disposed of his house and lot in Aberdeen, converting the proceeds into gold and bank notes, which while moths and rust might corrupt, Sheriffs could not pounce upon. Should such a thing as being 'pulled,' ever befall either of the Squires, they would undoubtedly have found some loop-hole through which to crawl out. Just where this loop-hole was has never been positively determined, although many are of the opinion that it was in the wording of the marriage ritual itself. That used by Beasley was as follows: 'My young friends, marriage is a solemn contract of plighted faith in holy wedlock, which is to last during your natural lives, as nothing but death shall sever your marriage vows. You will now please 'jine' your right hands. Do you both by virtue of your marriage vows pledge to each other your plighted faith in holy wedlock, to live, love, honor, and obey each other as a dutiful husband and wife thereby forsaking all others and living for each other alone till it shall please Almighty God in his providence to separate you both by death; to this do you both agree? (Answer). Inasmuch as you have plighted your faith in holy wedlock, the same being witnessed by an All-wise God and this audience here present, you may now legally and law-fully acknowledge yourselves as husband and wife. Take your seats'.

"Squire Shelton's service was much shorter and ran thus: 'Marriage is a solemn ordinance, instituted by an All-wise Jehovah. 'Jine' your right hands. Do you take this woman to nourish and cherish to keep her in sickness and health? (Answer). I hope you will live long and do well to-gether. Take your seats'. These are the words that have joined the lives of more than 20,000 couples. Squire Shelton read his ceremony in a loud, clear voice, while Squire Beasley mumbled his words in a low, inarticulate tone. These stereotyped forms never varied an iota with the exception of the last sentence in each 'Take Your Seats', was either add-ed or omitted as the occasion demanded. Squire Shelton's form had been objected to in that: it married the man to the woman, but not the woman to the man, all obligations being placed upon the husband's shoulders.

"The only people whoever said harm of Massie Beasley or who ever tried to do him serious injury, were the local members of the clerical profession on both sides of the River, who openly denounced him from their pulpits. But in spite of all their preaching and teaching against him, when any member of their congregation wanted to get married it was often Massie Beasley, and not the minister, who was favored with the job of tying the knot. One of the most bitter and vituperative denunciators of what he termed, 'This cry-ing evil in our midst' was a preacher who received a call to Aberdeen some few years before the Squire's death. This worthy man coaxed and pleaded, urged and exhorted, but to no avail. Wedding parties passed the parsonage door every day on their way to the Squire's and still the fees that by rights should have been to help swell the meager salary of the minister rolled into the already full and over-flowing coffer of the Merry Magistrate. At last, seeing that all his earnest exhortations of his flock were as seed sown on bar-ren ground, the discouraged parson decided to make a spe-cialty of the matrimonial business himself, seeing that there

238

was more money in it than in preaching the gospel. He was Massie Beasley's first and only rival and indeed was the only man who ever had the moral courage to attempt to wrest away what had been considered the perrogative of the Squire of Aberdeen for seventy-five years.

"The Minister introduced many new wrinkles into the business. Indeed he was obliged to do so in order to get a start. To this end, he cut rates and established agents at the ferry landing in Aberdeen and at the wharf and railroad stations in this city. Of course, the Squire was obliged to follow suit in order to keep abreast of the times. As a consequence, every couple who landed on ether side of the River, whether by ferry, steamboat or railroad, if they bore any evidence of being matrimonally inclined, were immediately pounced upon by these persistent drummers. The steamboats were thoroughly canvassed every time they made a landing here, and while efforts in this direction were scarcely ever immediately productive of good results, they were the means of influencing many a young man and woman from a distance to come to Aberdeen to be married. A large number of these steamboat customers came from the upper end of the River and were found usually on the Pittsburgh and Cincinnati Packet line boats. Each agent extolled the respective merits of his employer in the most persuasive language, giving his rival a metaphorical black eye. Beasley's agents represented that the Squire was the only person who was legally authorized to perform a marriage ceremony without a license, and that those performed by any other were bogus. The Parson's drummers made the same derogatory statements regarding Beasley's ceremonies.

"Sometimes, through a spirit of mischief, a wag of the town would wage that he could beguile a couple in search of the Squire into believing that he was the man, and actually marry them himself. His opportunity usually came when the Squire was absent at a county seat, where he was frequently called and whither he always went reluctantly. All Aberdeen folks were adept in spotting elopers, and it was not a difficult matter to find victims for the practical joker and his

239

boon companions. The selected couple were conducted to the tavern parlor where the presumptous was in wise and spectacles, was introduced to the green and bullible swains as the Squire of Aberdeen, who straightway performed the ceremony, signed their marriage certificate with the name of Massie Beasley, congratulated them and pocketed the fee. When the couple supposing themselves to be married had departed, the counterfeit Squire repaired to the barroom, collected his bets and spent the whole amount in treating the amused and amazed crowd. Incidents of this kind were, alas, of only too frequent occurence, and thus many people who are now trembling with the thought of having been married by Squire Beasley are even in more deplorable condition. Still 'where ignorance is bliss, 'tis folly to be wise,' and it would be an unkind thing to suggest that such persons compare the writing on their marriage certificates with the signature of Squire Beasley's.

"A visit last week to Squire Jesse Ellis, the gentleman to whom Squire Beasley willed his records and those of his predecessor, Thomas Shelton, was full of intense interest to me. Mr. Ellis has in his possession many unique relics of the late Squire, having served in the capacity of his deputy during the latter's decline. Through Mr. Ellis' courtesy I had the pleasure of looking over all the marriage records of Aberdeen since the day Shelton acceded to power on May 18, 1882, until Massie Beasley's death in 1892. They show the appearance of having been kept with a school girl nicety, and comprise nine ponderous volumes. What a prolific hotbed for campaign scandals, I thought to myself, as I turned the leaves of Squire Beasley's first volume and discovered the name of a man now of national, and indeed international, importance in politics. In my research through the yellow leaves of these musty, vellum-bound volumes and which was, moreover a very desultory and random one, I espied the names of five men who had occupied seats in the United States Congress; thirty-four men who have at some time or other filled the same position; seven ex-Senators of the United States, with one ex-Foreign Minister, Col. Thomas H.

240

Nelson of Terre Haute Indiana. Col. Nelson was Minister of Plenipotentiary to Chile under Abraham Lincoln and later under Hayes Administration; he was sent to Mexico on the same mission. The lady in the case was Miss Elizabeth Key, a lineal descendant of the author of "The Star Spangled Banner," and a representative of one of the oldest families of this city and State. How many people there are who have attained high political distinction and enviable social position since their marriages were recorded in these old books, it is impossible to estimate.

"There was a bit of pleasurable surprise in store for me when Mrs. Ellis called my attention to certain of Squire Beasley's documents, which, she proudly informed me had proven of so much interest to James Lane Allen, the Kentucky novelist who visited my host and hostess a little more than two years ago in search of data for his novel, "Butterflies." The elopement of Mr. Allen's hero and heroine, which it will be remembered brings the pretty story to a finish, was suggested to the author by various tales that he heard from Mrs. Ellis — the merry adventures and exploits of some of the bridal couples who sought the Squire of Aberdeen. Indeed, it was Squire Beasley himself who married Mr. Allen's Hilary and Daphne."

CHAPTER FIFTY-FIVE

FLEMING COUNTY SCHOOLS
Flemingsburg Kentucky

Listing of Superintendents for Fleming County Schools:

Milford Overley	1884-1891
W. G. Hart	1891-1895
C. G. Whaley	1895-1898
Lee N. Hull	1898-1906
Miss Anna Six	1906-1910
Mrs. Lutie Palmer Williams	1910-1914
L. N. Hull	1914-1918
Marvin Evans	1918-1944
Frank D. Scott	1944-1960
Arthur Cotterill	1960-1965
Charles A. Brown	1965———

CHAPTER FIFTY-SIX

FLEMING'S REPRESENTATIVES

The death of Raleigh Kendall Hart has caused some discussion as to the legislative representation of Fleming County and, from memory only we* give as far back as we can, and we think in their proper order the names of the men who have represented us.

In 1855 Landaff W. Andrews was elected and it was through his instrumentality that the County of Rowan was created thus settling the County seat controversy between Poplar Plains and Flemingsburg by the cutting off into the new County of all that territory lying between the East Fork of Triplett and the watershed which divides the waters of the North Fork of Triplett from the waters of Fox Creek. That section of the county was then rapidly settling up, and as Poplar Plains was then the terminus of the turnpike system, and largely the wholesale point for the mountain district with the wealth of the Kendalls, Pearces, Armstrongs, Logans, Harts and others to back her claims, she would undoubtedly have outvoted the western and northwestern end of the county and secured the county seat. Following L. W. Andrews in 1857, our memory does not serve us, but in 1859, Henry Bascon Dobyns was elected and we think the appended list is a correct one from that date on:

H. B. Dobyns	1859-61	Wm. J. Hendrick	1881-83
L. W. Andrews	1861-65	Raleigh K. Hart	1883-85
John M. Gray	1865-67	Jas. W. Crain	1885-87
Geo. M. Caywood	1867-69	Robert S. Hudson	1887-89
Francis R. Davis	1869-71	Enoch R. Burns	1889-91
Elisha A. Robertson	1871-73	Raleigh K. Hart	1891-95
Stephen R.		Oscar L. Hinton	1895-97
Campbell	1873-75	John S. Hood	1897-99
Hiram P. Jones	1875-77	Edwin M. Money	1899-03
James P. Allen	1877-79	Paul Heflin	1903-05
Robert H. Yantis	1879-81	Wm. M. Wilt	1905-07

Jno. T. Shanklin __ 1907-09   Chas. W. Fulton __ 1909-11
Sidney J. Collins _ 1911-13

The above was a clipping from The Times-Democrat. Hiram Duley,* Editor.

Sid J. Collins ____ 1912-14	H. W. McCartney _ 1942-44
J. D. Pumphrey __ 1914-18	C. D. (Jack) Call _ 1944-46
S. Lee McGohan _ 1918-20	S. J. Daugherty __ 1946-48
Chas. R. Scott ___ 1920-22	H. S. Overbey ___ 1948-50
Arthur Saunders _ 1922-26	True Mackey ____ 1950-52
J. R. Kelly _____ 1926-28	Herbert Fern ____ 1952-56
Jas. H. Muse ____ 1928-30	True Mackey ____ 1956-60
T. R. McRoberts _ 1930-32	Herbert F. Fern __ 1960-64
Sid J. Collins ___ 1932-36	Allie W. Young __ 1964-66
Lloyd McDonald _ 1936-38	Sherman Arnett __ 1966-72
Thomas Rigdon __ 1938-42	Austin Wenz ____ 1972-74

Dr. M. B. Denham   1974-

This information comes from Kentucky Directories, Kentucky House Journal, Kentucky Senate Journal, and the Courier Journal. Some variations were found in spelling and initials.

Printed in the USA
CPSIA information can be obtained
at www.ICGtesting.com
LVHW090253041023
759837LV00005B/990